BUSHMORE'S DARK SECRETS

PETER EDWARDS

PETER EDWARDS

ISBN 978-0-9945133-1-1

Also by Peter Edwards,

ALL MINE

a story of obsession

Follow me on Instagram
peteredwardsallmine

Website: allminestories.com
Email: allminestories@bigpond.com

Liked my book, then please like my page,

www.facebook.com/PeterEdwardsAuthor

Twitter: Peter Edwards@allminestories

PETER EDWARDS

BUSHMORE'S DARK SECRETS

For Sol and Jenn.

PETER EDWARDS

PROLOGUE

2015

My son Jack fell a long way last night. Nurse Blaxland called soon after breakfast. He wasn't expected to make it through the day, so our family gathered at Jack's holiday home and travelled to the district hospice together.

His brother Tommy visited along with Jack's dearest friends, Nick and his partner Cherub. His three children, young Jack, Lucy and Denise all said their heartfelt goodbyes while I was out of the room. He conditioned them as best he could for his impending death, telling them his passing would become an important part of their lives, but was adamant he didn't want his children to see him finally succumb. Although my grandchildren wanted to be present, they knew there was no further discussion to be had. Once my son made up his mind it was final.

I watched his laboured breathing. Even my eyes hurt, such was the pain of seeing my eldest boy die. The only thing this disease hadn't taken yet was his soul.

He cut his visits four weeks ago and things have been nice and quiet since, but before that time Jack accepted his many friends with all the typical bulldog tenacity he displayed throughout his life. I reckon half the golf club came through to pay their respects along with yachtsmen and business associates from around the country. They stood alongside plumbers who had worked with him and for him over the years. Many of Melbourne's leading thoroughbred racing identities came too; jockeys, trainers, even other owners. Most were people from the other side of money who he rarely spoke of to me. I'm just an old retired plumber with a crook back and a liver as useless as tits on a bull, but I was touched deeply by how they all spoke of my son.

The door opened, his wife Wendy entered and sat down. Her face drawn, her eyes dry. Relief will be a welcome stranger for her, too. We held one boney hand each listening to the rasping of air into tired, spent lungs. He cracked his eyes open and raised a finger, pointing to the bag on the chair beside Wendy.

'Take a look,' she said.

I opened the bag and saw the back of a thick, yellow clip folder full of paper, about a half ream in thickness. I ignored it and slid out the leather satchel with his MacBook inside, although I wondered where he'd find the strength in those fingers to push the keys. I passed the laptop over.

'No,' he mouthed.

'No?'

'No.' The finger moved down.

'The folder?'

I held it up, the lips moved, air hissed. 'Yeah, Dad.'

Wendy nodded and I opened the folder and read the first page.

ENOUGH ROPE
BY
JACK GILLINGS

'Shit Jack! No … no.' I glared at him in disbelief. For a brief second I saw a monster. Then I looked harder and saw my son, Jack. It was still my beautiful boy beneath those eyes, sunk deep behind the protruding cheekbones below them.

'Jack … how did this get in here?'

I turned toward Wendy. Surely she didn't know. But I could tell from her compressed, flattened out lips that she did. She kept a strict eye on what came and went from her husband's room.

'Linda,' Wendy said.

Then I recalled Jack's secretary had paid a visit yesterday afternoon.

'You've read this?'

'Not this one,' Wendy said. 'I ran my eyes over an edited version, one with a happy ending he and a publisher worked on sometime around the late nineties. They changed a lot of stuff, to make a better story and all that but Jack pulled the plug. Couldn't go through with it. This is the original manuscript he wrote back in '83, the year after it happened. He kept it in his safe.'

'Why ... why now? We left all this behind.'

'He never could,' Wendy said. 'We've been speaking. He always thought he'd have the time to maybe ... maybe find the right moment to give it to you. Other times I thought he'd never really get around to it, but these last weeks, this illness has changed his mind. He wants you to know everything. The truth.'

'And Nick?'

She shook her head. 'Jack said it's for you to read, then he wants you to destroy it. I have always asked him never to show you but he's made his decision. You know our Jack.'

'We buried this years ago ... when we left that town.' I looked to my son and he said one more ghostly word, 'Read.'

I pulled my glasses from my pocket and slipped them on. The next page was blank except for his handwritten words,

FOR MUM, DAD AND TOMMY.

PETER EDWARDS

CHAPTER 1

1983

My name is Jack Gillings. I am sixteen years old at writing and directly responsible for the deaths of two people. I live with my family in the coastal town of St Claire on the Great Ocean Road in Victoria's southwest. We moved here just under a year ago, but I grew up in another country town called Bushmore, slightly inland about a half hour drive to the northeast, high up in the Otway Ranges.

In Bushmore, we lived at 19 Pinehurst Avenue. St Patrick's Secondary College was my school, but not by choice. I wanted to be at the Bushmore High School where my mates were and where the girls went.

I hated my school with a passion.

Christian Brothers ran St Pat's. When it came to being strict, those weirdos were full on. Our first punishment of every morning was that classes began at eight forty, sharp, twenty minutes before my mates began their lessons at high school. Then they'd try and control your life at every turn, even coming to and from school. Teachers would deliberately drive past the bus stop and if we weren't wearing ties or blazers, then lookout. Hell … you might've just loosened your tie to get a bit of relief from the heat, or your socks were down, scrunched around your ankles, it didn't matter. We'd get detention. They even used spotters, usually senior kids to report us for so called *uniform crimes* on the bus. They'd ram religious education down our throats every day. Then came the daily grind of two to three hours of homework, and a minimum of three, sometimes four hours on weekends. As if six and a half hours a day stuck in school, five days a week for six years of my life wasn't enough time for them to do their jobs properly. It seemed to be enough time for high school teachers – none of my mates copped any homework at all.

Each morning I'd try and smash out my homework while stuffing down breakfast in my room, because there was simply too many fun things for a fourteen-year-old to do after school in Bushmore. I'd either be motorbike riding, hanging out at my mates houses, playing the pinnies in the pinball parlour or even roof-rocking teachers houses after dark. Anything but homework.

English, History, Geography and P.E. were the only subjects that interested me, all the rest were totally unnecessary for my future. I'd already decided to be a plumber like my dad. I knew the job inside out. I'd been working with him for most of my life and my oldies both agreed I could begin my apprenticeship with Dad after year ten. Meaning, at the time of the events in this story, I only had another year and a term to go.

And that's where I have to begin. A little over one year ago on the second last day of mid-term in 1982, when Tony Debono clobbered me good and proper on the school bus for the final time.

Each morning I'd walk to Ackley Street, three streets away from my home and catch the bus from there. Debono hopped on the bus at Pinehurst Avenue. I know it might sound strange – Debono and I lived only three houses apart – but there were two reasons why I walked to Ackley Street every morning.

Firstly, Debono was a year older and had picked on me since our late primary school years. Before that time we grew up together, messing around in the street and at each other's houses. Then he changed and became an arsehole and now, I didn't even want to stand next to him at the bus stop. The second reason was so I could walk Rex, my border collie in the mornings. *"Your dog, your responsibility"*, Mum always said. Once I was on the bus, Rex would make his way home and then walk with my younger brother, Tommy to the primary school.

To avoid Debono, I'd try to find a seat as far down the back of the bus as possible. If he passed me down the aisle, I risked being clipped on the way through. Most times it was only a slap under the chin or over the side of the head, the odd knuckle grind through the hair, that sort of thing. Not enough to hurt too much, just enough to piss me off and push my boundaries as far as he could. Sometimes I'd be lucky and find a corner spot in the back seat where he couldn't reach me. Other times I'd kick a skin nut (year seven kid) out of a window seat and made him sit next to the aisle.

But on that particular day the second school bus had broken down, meaning the kids from Beaconshire – the nearest town to ours – filled the back of our bus. I'd been forced to take up an aisle seat half way down. Debono got on and began calling out stuff and whooping and hollering to his mates down the back. He hardly had any mates in Bushmore, yet he seemed to get along with the kids from Beaconshire. (I figured they didn't know how much of a dickhead he really was outside of school.) Then he saw me, and that stupid grin widened. He wore a gold stud in his left ear. What a tosser. He'd have to take it out before school otherwise he'd get detention, but most kids had sussed him out long ago as a spotter which explained how he got away with wearing the earring on the bus.

As he approached me down the aisle, I had my hands ready to cover my ears where he clipped me last time.

'Gillo,' he said in a smartarse voice. I watched him carefully as he passed, thinking I was in the clear because he had his eyes up, grinning at his mates down the back. Then the left hand shot out and palmed me on the forehead, ramming my head into the chrome steel bar that looped over the top of the seat. The blow knocked my senses around a bit and I saw red. At almost fifteen years of age, I'd had enough.

'Fuck you,' I screamed and went totally ape shit. I leapt into the aisle and punched the back of his head so hard it sent him stumbling forward. I shook my hand, the centre knuckle felt like it might be broken. He tried to spin around but with his school bag on his back, the aisle was too narrow. I had one chance to keep going so I ignored the pain and with both hands reefed his head by the hair, dragging him down onto the floor of the bus. I stomped on his head and as he tried to get back up, I bent down and thumped him one more time right in the earhole before the bus brakes squealed and the big hands of George, the Greek bus driver hauled me back up the aisle by the scruff of the neck.

Voices were egging me on yelling, 'Gillo Gillo.' Others urged Debono on but the fight was over in a flash. Of course I knew George would report us both; I didn't care. It felt good to be cheered and this prick had been bullying me for way too long. I liked George. He knew the history between Debono and myself and made me sit up the front and sent Debono to the back for the rest of the journey. I'd kicked his arse and that was worth the Saturday morning detention we both knew was coming our way. Debono was bigger and stronger than me and I knew I was in for it and would spend the school holidays looking over my shoulder each time I left the house. But as I said earlier, that was the last time he ever belted me because soon after, Tony Debono would be dead and I was responsible.

CHAPTER 2

Spring arrived in the first week of the holidays, flourishing our corner of the Otways. Flourishing. A word my mum often used to describe spring, her favourite time of year when she said God's hand flourished everything.

Those school holidays were awesome because I met Old Nick, the legendary wild man of the bush who had set up camp in our end of the Otways forest, sometime through August. For the last two weeks of term Old Nick's name was on the lips of every kid at school and around town.

At the time, I was bored and looking for something to do. Our footy season was over for the year. Mum made me play for the school and we finished bottom of the ladder without winning a game. I played full back. Twenty-two goals were kicked over my head in the final game and I was glad to see the end of that season. Our Principal, Brother Hobbins coached us and he couldn't coach a fly to land on a shit bag in the afternoon sun, as my dad would say. Dad also often made a comment on my own football ability, saying I'd never make a footballer as long as my arsehole pointed to the ground. I didn't appreciate it, even though it was true. Being a plumber, my old man had some great sayings.

On Saturday I watched the Bushmore seconds lose their preliminary final and listened to the radio as North Melbourne flogged my side, Essendon in the big league, knocking us out of the finals. Just like Dad said they would. Sunday, I went to church with Mum and Tommy, (the second I turned eighteen and got my motorbike license, I planned to never go to church again) then I spent the afternoon riding motorbikes with my mates, Neil *Roddy* Rodwell, Brett *Meatlips* Thornton, Paul

Cudgy Cudgesell and Glenn Trimble, aka *Soupy*. At the time we were all best mates. Later in the year they would become my accomplices, and then, my arch-enemies.

The first Monday of the holidays came around quickly and I decided to go down to find Old Nick's camp for myself, without telling anyone.

To most people, Old Nick was a vagrant, a loner to be wary of. I saw him as a mythical creature who moved about to all different parts of the forest. Last time he camped near Bushmore I was nine. (I remember hearing of him camping on this side of the Otways one time before but I can't quite recall my age.) Naturally, at the time our oldies warned us to leave him alone and banned us from entering the forest, but we were adventurous nine-year-olds and just starting to find out they couldn't keep an eye on us all the time. Roddy, Meatlips, Cudgy and myself (Soupy hadn't moved into town yet) found his camp but we only dared to go near it once, just close enough to see. We'd heard rumours he'd shot at other kids with a slug gun – some said a 22 rifle – and at that age, we believed it and got out of there pretty quick, swearing never to return.

Then one day after that summer he packed up and vanished without a trace. We guessed he'd gone to another section of the forest. Now I was much older and had Rex with me, and a compass.

I pedalled into the forest on the Laxby Road and left my bike in the long grass of the roadside culvert, then walked through the bush in the vicinity of where I'd heard he might be. After two hours I found his camp in the bottom of a valley beside a creek. From the top of a ridge overlooking his shack, I watched him go about his business. He'd walk down to the creek for water, tend to potted plants around his camp and then disappear back into his shack. Each time he came out I grabbed Rex by the collar and crouched behind a tree. I reckon I was at least a hundred metres away up the slope, when he appeared and began pulling clothes off the rope line. I moved several feet to my right to get a better view from behind another tree, that's all it took for him to look up and shield the sun with his hands. He stared straight up the ridge at me.

I ran like shit out of a shanghai down the opposite slope. That was another saying my dad used all the time. He called a slingshot a shanghai. Whenever he saw something going quick – a car, a boat, motorbike, whatever – he would say, *"Wow ... look at that thing go, like shit out of a shanghai."* I reckon he had that saying arse about. I'd never tried it, but I certainly couldn't see shit going fast out of a shanghai. Some of it would even stick in the leather pouch, for sure. Anyway, I bolted over the back of the ridge as fast as I could go, leaping over tree stumps and logs, hoping not to break a leg or an ankle in the animal scratchings. Palm fronds and grass stalks on the black boys flicked against my clothes, stinging my hands. I reached the gully at the bottom of the next valley and dived into a clump of bushes, shit scared. Holding Rex tight, I caught a breath. My skin tingled with fear but there was also a wild sense of excitement running through me. I looked for him between the branches, picturing him stalking me, gun raised, ready to shoot but despite the rumours, I knew he wouldn't shoot at a kid, surely.

No one came. After several minutes Rex started getting restless and began a low whine. I had to move so I took a chance and sprang through the bush and up the side of the next hill, always looking behind, listening to every sound other than my panting and my own feet tearing through the bush, worrying that Old Nick would circle me and jump out in front. Exhausted, I made it to my bike and got the hell out of there, but curiosity drove me back. Next day I found his camp a lot easier, taking under an hour to reach the ridge from the road. I hid in a different spot and watched, locked in both fascination and fear.

In the afternoon he went for a walk through the forest toward the river. Rex and I followed from a distance. This time I saw the gun. A strange weapon with a handle similar to a shotgun, although it seemed shorter and didn't have a barrel. More like a spear gun. I couldn't really tell because he held it in front, pointing toward the ground. He also carried a fishing rod and a bucket.

I watched him for maybe a little over an hour; close enough to hear the river running crisp over a fall at the end of the pool he fished in. Close enough to see he wore a woollen jacket with a thick collar, kind of like my dad's Starsky jacket although Old Nick's one was brown, not white and didn't have different patterns on the arms and waist. Perhaps it was a home-made job. Dad and I watched Starsky and Hutch and C.H.iP.s every week, our two favourite cop shows and like every kid in Bushmore, I wanted a Starsky jacket. Dad owned one and Mum said we couldn't afford to have two, so I'd wear Dad's whenever we watched the show.

Old Nick caught a trout; a good-sized fish too from what I could see. A short time later he was gone. I was probably day-dreaming, (I don't really know) but I'd taken my eyes off him and when I looked back up he was no longer beside the river. I crouched down and waited. We weren't near his camp so I wasn't so scared anymore. Then I saw movement to my right. Old Nick slipped through the trees maybe twenty metres away. I could see an arched bow in the top of the gun. A crossbow? I'd never seen one up close, only on the mail order coupons and advertisements in my uncle Laurie's hunting mags. I held Rex by the collar, he whined loudly. My head shot up to see Old Nick still walking; he didn't appear to have heard Rex. I placed my other hand over my dog's jaws and said, 'Shhhh.' I think he understood because he stayed as still as a sleeping bat, licking my palm while the wild-man of the Otways passed by.

I followed him towards his shack. I had to. It was also the way back to my bike, otherwise I might have gotten lost in those valleys because I forgot to keep checking my compass. Staying well out of sight, my plan was to skirt his camp and keep going before the sun fell. Then all of a sudden, I lost him again. Gone. Disappeared in a gully. I heard another trickling stream nearby and noticed the lush green vegetation down the slope. On the other side, I saw his shack. He'd led me back a different way and was nowhere to be seen. The forest took on its usual late afternoon chill. Wind dropped and the sun was about to disappear over the ridge, lengthening the shadows around me. Something made a dull thud to my far left up the slope. Rex yelped and bolted off into the scrub. I assumed he was after a rabbit or a wallaby. Alone, I watched him dodging the trunks, unable to call his name. The clunk of iron jaws snapping together hit the air, scaring the life out of me. Twigs and leaves in front of me sprang up as my hand thumped my chest.

He stepped out from behind a tree to my right (I had no idea how he did it). I grabbed the tree trunk behind with both hands, staring back at his cunning, scary eyes which bore down on me from between his tangled light brown hair and the mass of his grubby, wiry beard. He held up a stick with the rabbit trap clamped shut over the end. The fishing rod and the fish were both gone. In his other hand he held the cross bow with a trigger handle, same as a shotgun. I stared at the arrow, then at him.

'You've been watching me for two days, young fella,' he said in a clear voice like out of a radio. I hadn't expected such a friendly tone. Even still I was terrified. My hands trembled so I shoved them deep into my jeans pockets, not knowing if he'd shoot me in the back if I dared to run.

No, of course he wouldn't.

I stood positively still as Rex came running back, barking wildly. Old Nick knelt down with one knee lower than the other and eased the cross bow and the stick with the rabbit trap onto the ground. To my relief I noticed the string on the weapon wasn't tensioned up. He held the back of his right hand forward. Rex approached, snarling and baring his fangs. His body shuddered beneath his black and white coat. He let out two more cautious barks, trying to bluff the guy, but Old Nick didn't flinch. Rex then turned to me and twisted his head. He did that when he was confused, he'd never attacked anyone.

'What's your dog's name, son?' He flashed a concerning smile, and instantly I saw he had good teeth, white and straight.

I tried to say Rex but my throat was dry and my voice wouldn't work. I swallowed a couple of times before I could speak. 'Rex.'

'Rex huh. Be a good boy then, Rex.'

Rex gave a high-pitched whine and sniffed the back of his hand. Old Nick stroked him, settling my dog with ease. 'There's a good boy. Imagine if your dog's foot got caught in that trap, I'd have to put him down on the spot, unless … unless you've got it in you.'

'No.'

'You want him killed?'

'No.'

'There's traps all round here son, dangerous place for a boy and a dog.' Rex licked his hand and Old Nick ruffled the fur on his head, then picked up the weapon and stood. He wore flared denims; they were filthy. Nobody wore flares anymore. (I hadn't worn them for years.) I guessed him to be a little shorter than my dad, maybe six foot one or two, and lean with good square shoulders, the kind I hoped to have when I was older. Lately I'd been pumping weights in my room, although more often than not I either forgot or found something better to do. 'So why are you following me around?'

A gust of wind sprang from nowhere. I stared down at the trap, then at the crossbow, yet I realised I had nothing to fear from this guy.

'I ... I wanted to meet you.'

'Why?'

I gulped. 'To learn how to fish and hunt ... properly like you do.'

'Do you now? S'pose you want me to teach you?'

I did, despite being too terrified to ask.

'Normally when kids come down here, they come in groups, causing me loads of problems.'

'Do you—?' Really shoot at them, I wanted to ask but fear locked my tongue again.

I must have been staring at the bow because he said, 'What?' His eyes lit up, he lifted the bow. 'Shoot at 'em.' Then he laughed. 'I've heard the rumours. Course not. Don't even own a gun. Just yell at 'em, tell 'em to shove off. They get bored and leave me alone after a while.'

'And who are you, then?'

'Huh?

'Your name? Got a name, son?'

'Jack,' I said through gibbering, dry lips. 'Jack Gillings.'

A big hand shot out, fingers fanned open and we shook hands. 'Nick. You drink tea, Jack?'

Tea was just what I needed and he invited me into his shack. Rex and I both liked him straight away and I think he liked me from that moment too. Rather than being scared, I actually felt excited going into his shack. It was basic. Three walls, one window, no glass of course, just flywire nailed tight over an opening. Heavy green tent cloth, like army issue served as a flap door. A potbelly stove stood against a sidewall. Bundled kindling was stacked across the back wall next to a rolled up swag tucked in the corner. Furniture was a tree stump and a square table, like the one we folded out to play cards on at home. As he moved about he ducked beneath utensils and pans, strung on wire across the centre of the room along with clumps of garlic and rabbit skins. Above the kindling I noticed one shelf about a foot long. It wasn't really a shelf, just a short plank with two long nails driven beneath it for support. A small wooden box sat on top. It had gold and black squares like a draughts board; only the board Tommy and I played on had white and black squares.

He must have noticed me staring again.

'You play chess?'

Only the two brainiac Chinese kids, a year below me at school played chess and they had to play the teachers because nobody else cared.

'Nah. Play draughts but.'

'Well then, one day you gotta step up, play a real game.' He chuckled with an evil, fun type of grin. 'A game of war.'

'War?' I'd always thought of chess being too hard, too nerdy. Not war.

'Oh yeah. There's no game in the world that matches wits like chess.' He reached up and handed me down the box. It was heavy. 'Open it.'

I unlatched the clips. The inside was lined with blue felt material like I'd seen on pool tables in American movies. Neatly sitting in tight little pockets were white and black shiny pieces all facing the same way. The white pieces had orange, rustic streaks and the black figures had white streaks and gold speckles through the stone.

'Crafted from Italian marble,' he said. 'The box is mahogany. Handmade. My father bought me this set when I won the school championship at thirteen years of age. Even knocked off the senior kids.'

'I've never seen marble before.'

'Can't say that tomorrow, son.'

'Huh?' Then I clicked. 'Oh yeah. Totally.'

'Wait here.' He disappeared out the flap and rolled in another stump for me to sit on. Then he laid the board and the pieces out with care and began to teach me the set up and how each piece moved. As I watched and listened, I became confused with the names of the pieces and their odd directions. No way was I going to remember it all, but I gained a little confidence in this short period of time, enough to ask him who he really was and how he came to live in the forest.

He gave me a relaxed smile and said, 'There are some things a boy just doesn't need to know.'

I knew I'd gone too far because it sounded like something one of my teachers, Mr. Trellard would say when he wanted to ice a student's line of annoying questions. As we played what he called a mock game, he also gave me a warning.

'I don't mind you coming down here. Guess you didn't roof rock my hut or steal anything. You seem like a good kid and I could do with a game every now and then. If you want to learn chess or hunting, fishing, whatever, I don't mind teaching you anything, but don't bring any of your mates around and if there's no smoke coming from that flue pipe, don't come down here. What'd I just say?'

'Huh?'

'No smoke—'

'Don't come down here.'

'Good boy. And part of the deal is you have to tell your parents where you are.'

I agreed, even though it sucked. My pairs would never approve of me coming here and if they asked where I'd been, I'd have to lie.

As it turned out, when I got home I told them nothing because they didn't ask. They must have assumed I'd been hanging out with my mates.

I visited Nick the next day and brought a bag of sultanas and a half a dozen lemons off our tree. Rain began to pelt down once I was halfway through the forest so I ran the rest of the way to the shack, glad to see smoke rising from the flue. When the rain stopped, it still dripped in an offbeat, heavy patter from the overhead trees and we were forced to talk loud for a while as we ate sultanas and drank home-made herbal tea, while trying to play his crazy war game. I became fascinated at how the different pieces moved in so many strange ways and set my mind to learn chess, no matter what. He asked a lot of questions about me and the only info I gained on him was his age, thirty-six – same as my dad – not that old for a guy known as Old Nick. I suppose he just seemed older. Maybe it was the way his beard grew so high on his cheekbones.

'Do your parents know you're down here?'

'Nope. Haven't told them.' I didn't want to lie to him.

He rubbed his beard for a few seconds. 'Today's Wednesday, right?'

I nodded.

'By Friday, the bad weather should be passed. I'll take you fishing, but only if you tell them where you are. If you want to come, be here early Friday morning. Eight o'clock. If your parents say it's okay, I got no problem. Otherwise, don't come back, ever. Sound fair?'

I nodded again, knowing it meant trouble. Dad *might* be okay but it was a long shot. Mum, definitely not. Forget about it. There would not be a right moment to tell her in a month of Sundays. Could they really stop me from going into the forest anymore? Christ, I was nearly fifteen and able to make my own decisions. Nick and I were becoming mates and I began to think of how I'd tell Dad what a great guy Nick really was. I knew Dad would get along with him, too.

While riding my bike home that evening, all I could think about was Old Nick and how he wasn't anything like the ogre people thought he was. Most of the rumours only came from other kids anyway, either at school or down at the pinball shop in the main street. After living in a small town all my life, why was I still surprised when rumours turn out to be complete bullshit?

CHAPTER 3

Friday morning I worked with Dad and couldn't go fishing early with Old Nick. I didn't get back out to his camp until after lunch. When I rounded the top of the ridge, I became both relieved and surprised to see smoke rising from the potbelly stove, meaning I didn't have to walk to the river to find him.

On my way down the valley, the sight of a huge red kangaroo skin hanging off a tree confronted me. Then as I got nearer, the smell hit. A rank stench surrounded me as huge blowflies attacked in swarms. I fought them off and saw what they were going buzz crazy about. Rex was sniffing a pile of intestines and organs lumped on the ground several feet from the back wall of the shack. 'Get away from that,' I said, and noticed a severed roo's head, which blended in with the black soil and foliage of the forest floor, eyes staring to nowhere. I dry-retched with my hand over my mouth to avoid swallowing a fly, then ran around to the front.

'Nick,' I called, almost choking.

'Come in, young Jack.'

'Stay here,' I said to Rex and rested my fishing rod against the wall, then pushed the flap aside and entered. He was butchering up the roo on an old table that took up half his shack.

'How do you like this big fella?'

'Choice.'

'Got him right on dusk last night. Managed to get close enough to put a bolt through the chest. Got lucky too. The mob was heading toward my camp. And, see that pile of guts out there on your way in?'

'How could I miss it?'

He chuckled. 'The roo dropped dead halfway up that slope behind the hut. I was able to rope him and drag him down and gut him, otherwise I would've had to wait for you to help me.'

That made me feel good. 'Why not clean it up?'

He grinned and held his arms wide. 'What do you see?'

I looked around. 'A dead roo?'

'What else … what don't you see?'

'What—?' Then it hit me. 'No flies.'

'Hey Jack, well done, they're all too busy out there. First lesson for the day. Create a diversion. Thought we were fishing this morning?' He didn't turn around, just kept on hacking at the meat.

'Had to work with Dad. Hope you didn't hang around waiting?'

'Ahhh, not too fussed, got plenty to do.'

He had a pile of steaks already cut up. Ribs and bones bloodied the table. 'What you gonna do with all that meat?'

He chuckled and said, 'Bung it in the freezer.'

'Yeah right! What freezer?' (I actually looked around and felt rather stupid).

'One of those things a boy don't need to know.' He flashed a broad grin I was fast becoming accustomed to. 'So you told your parents?'

'Yeah, they're totally cool.' It was only a part lie. I didn't want to tell Nick what Bushmore's finest Catholic (as Dad called Mum) really thought of a fourteen year-old boy visiting an old hobo in the Otways. I did tell them last night and I also picked the opportune time – what I thought was my opportune time, not theirs – while Mum and I were cleaning up after dinner. Dad was in a rush because every Thursday, the Bushmore Pub ran a happy hour between six and eight and he wanted to be there for the meat raffle. After a brief conversation, I got my cold answer, "*No*," before Dad left and Mum lectured me while I dried the dishes.

Once again I'd done the right thing and told the truth, and once again the truth had brought me undone. Honesty's supposed to be the best policy, so much for that bullshit. I agreed not to go back to Nick's camp. With Mum, I really had no choice. When she told me to do something, I usually agreed knowing it was easier and then I'd end up doing what I wanted to do anyway, and simply lie to cover my tracks. Just like any normal fourteen year-old country kid.

'She said it's fine as long as I bring Rex and I'm home for dinner. Said to give you this, too.' I reached into my backpack and handed him the jar of plum jam.

He folded his arms and gave only a slight nod. I think he totally sussed me out for bullshitting, but said, 'All right. As long as you told her, and tell her I said thank you too, son. Lemons were good.'

I wished I *could* tell her, I thought as I unzipped one of the side pockets. 'Brought some cheddar, too.'

He stared at the cheese in my hand. 'Hey … I appreciate it, but you don't have to bring me food.'

'I don't mind.' And I didn't really because I reckoned it was fair. I wanted to learn so much off him.

Rex poked his head through the flap. Nick gave him a thighbone and he disappeared.

'Know how to use a stone?' He spun around with the blade of the long boning knife facing toward me, holding a rectangle sharpening stone in the other hand.

'Totally,' I said.

'All right, give that a quick sharpen for me.'

I began to run the blade over the stone.

'Ten degrees, ten degrees … you're holding it too high. Hold it flatter. Like this.' He showed me what ten degrees was. 'Who the hell ever taught you that? Ten degrees and ten times on each side.'

'Dad reckons twenty degrees.'

'Hate to tell you son, Daddy's wrong.' He had this big grin on his face. I handed him back the knife when I finished and he kept carving the meat up.

'You hungry?'

'Totally starvin'. Had lunch but … been a long walk.'

'Fire that pan up then.'

I put the pan on the potbelly and he chucked on a couple of steaks, cut thin, and then he sprinkled his home grown mixed herbs on top with garlic and onions. He told me the names of the different herbs, some of which I knew like basil and lemon thyme. Then there's tarragon, he called that the king of all herbs.

He held up a leaf, the same green colour as spearmint. 'Sage. Know what sage is?'

'Nope.'

'A powerful herb. "How can a man die with sage in his garden," is an old Arab saying.'

'Never heard of it.'

'Can't say that tomorrow, son.'

'What? Oh yeah, guess you're right.' He kept springing that on me.

I'd tasted roo steaks before, not as good as Old Nick cooked them. Afterwards we went outside where he moved a stack of earthenware pots to reveal a grubby old hessian cloth covering the dirt. He lifted the cloth. Underneath was the lid of a large steel car fridge buried in the ground. The freezer? He packed the rest of the meat in the esky, padlocked it and then dug a hole out the back and buried the remains of the kangaroo before we went fishing for the afternoon. We trekked through the bush along the river and found a different water hole where we caught two trout. He got one and I got one, both caught on my cheese.

On the way back he began to teach me how to read time and direction from the sun. Of course I already knew the points of the compass, but Nick prided himself on not having to use one in the forest. When we got back to the camp he noticed something wrong straight away and spent a few tense moments searching around, inside and outside.

'Someone's been here.'

'How can you tell?' Then I noticed him studying footprints.

'Look here. Different treads to yours, plus check your dog out. He's found a fresh scent, maybe a smell he already knows.'

It was true. Rex had his nose to the ground, sniffing about, wagging his tail. Nick seemed to know my dog better than me.

'You tell any of your mates you been coming down here?'

'Nope. Just my pairs.'

'You sure? Would they tell any of your mates' parents … I mean, that way your mates might find out. Cause whoever's been here is a kid on his own. Someone's followed you.' He seemed a little agitated and I became worried he'd pay out on me.

'No way.' I shook my head. 'No one's followed me.'

'Yeah, all right … can't see anything missing.' He didn't seem all too convinced and gave a suspicious, sideways glance, the same as he had earlier when I lied to him about what I'd told my oldies. 'Next week we'll head to the coast, do some real fishing huh, what do you say?'

'Sounds good, but how do we get there? I can bring my motorbike, but—'

'Don't worry about that, just ride your pushy. Don't want trail bikes around here. What do you reckon, meet here seven a.m. Tuesday, if the weather's good. Have a full belly and bring some lunch for yourself, we'll be gone most of the day.'

'Catch you then.' My mind was already beginning to churn over the lies I'd have to tell Mum. Where could I say I was heading that early in the morning?

Luckily I had a plastic bag in my backpack, so I wrapped the trout up, grabbed my rod and walked out of the forest only to find out my bike was gone, stolen. Someone *had* followed me. Knobby treads and skid marks in the gravel were from a motorbike. I had a fair idea Debono was the culprit.

CHAPTER 4

A mist had descended over Whispering Creek, which cut through the bush behind all the houses in Pinehurst Avenue. As I made my way in the fading light along the track on top of the embankment, I was so pissed off. Rex and I had walked the entire way home. Friday night was fish and chip night and I thought it might be nice for Mum to have fresh fish with her chips. Now I was in strife for being late, just my luck. The blocks in our street were all a half-acre in size and I reached the Debono's property first. Mr. Debono was working up behind the house in the front part of his vegetable garden, beside the large hothouse Dad helped him build a couple of years ago.

'Mr. Gillings,' he bellowed in his jovial Italian accent as he saw me climbing through his wire fence. When he said *"Mr. Gillings"* he sort of had this musical tone to his voice that made me smile. He was a nice man and preferred us kids to call him by his first name, which was also Tony. But Mum made me call him Mr. Debono. So in his humorous way, he called me Mr. Gillings back and all the other kids by their first names. Their oldies didn't care about useless formalities.

'Hi Mr. Debono. Take a look at this.' I reached into my backpack and held up the trout.

'Fish! You bring 'a me fish? Ahhh, you good boy, Mr. Gillings.'

'Nah. It's for Mum.'

'Oh well, nex'a time you catch 'a one for me.'

'No problem. I owe you a fish then.' It was the least I could do. All of Dad's tomatoes came from Mr. Debono's seedlings.

Tony came out the back door, sporting a familiar, false cheesy grin. He still owed me one big-time for embarrassing him in front of his mates. Our school broke up for holidays on the Thursday afternoon so neither of us got Saturday morning detention. Instead we were both required for three hours on the Friday morning, first day of the holidays.

My bike leaned against their side fence. 'You totally pinched my bike.'

'Found it in the grass on the Laxby Road. Thought you might—'

'As if you didn't know it's mine, arsehole.'

His scowl surfaced, it was never too far away. The right corner of his lips lifted and his sharp eyes gleamed *"fuck you."*

'You're lucky I found it. Tyres are flat.'

'Funny that.'

'Yeah heah, funny that.' He thrust his chin up and sniffed. He had a habit of sniffing. 'You racing Sunday?'

'What's it to you?' We raced motorbikes around the rim of the abandoned quarry down off Dartmoore Road, mostly on Sunday afternoons. My mates and I formed a club about a year ago, the Bushmore Motocross Club and we wouldn't let him join. (He'd threatened to burn our clubhouse down when we told him.) Debono was the only other kid who rode at the quarry, most kids rode at the Mackie's farm, west of the town. The Mackie boys went to my school. Debono used to ride with them until he got caught shoplifting from their dad's hardware store in the main street. Now he was trying to suck up to us so he can have someone to ride with.

'You're full of shit,' he said. 'Rode with Roddy and Soupy today, they said you guys are racing Sunday.'

'Your fuckin' bullshit meter's totally blown a fuse, wanker.'

'Yeah, then how'd I know you're racing?'

I shrugged. 'Don't mean I'll be racing.' Instantly I became pissed off again. They're supposed to be my mates. They knew the club rules and they weren't allowed to tell him when the races were on.

He sniffed again. 'You hanging out with Old Nick tomorrow then?'

Now I hated him even more.

'Catch, Mr. Gillings.' Mr. Debono called and I turned to see a jar of plum jam hurtling through the air toward me. I caught it and smiled at him, glad for the interruption.

'Your mother, she 'a ring before, said she run out. Bring eighty cents tomorrow.'

'Sure, Mr. Debono.' Darkness was falling over and the mist was beginning to morph into a thick pea soup, so I began pushing my bike past Debono out to the street.

'What'll your old chook say if she finds you been hanging out with the forest creep?'

I stopped and turned; resigned to the fact he would tell my mum. She actually liked Tony. I think she felt sorry for him. The half-smile half-scowl buckled his lips.

'Bet your olds told you not to go down there, didn't they?'

I couldn't answer, but promised myself to pump more weights so I could hit him harder next time. I'd felt strong on the bus.

'Knew so,' he said. 'Wait'll I tell 'em.'

'Come on. No need to—'

'He only joking,' Mr. Debono said and we both turned. Now he stood only a few feet away, waiving a finger in the air. 'He not 'a say anything to your parents. I make sure.'

I smiled at him. He knew exactly what was going on. I often wondered how such a kind-hearted man could have such an arsehole for a son. I held up the jam. 'See you tomorrow, Mr. Debono. Suck shit,' I whispered to Tony before I walked my bike up the street to my house. Dad had the light on in the shed with the bonnet of his work ute raised.

My dad's a great dad, just drinks a bit. That's his vice, but he also worked hard and had a great sense of humour. *"Work is the curse of the drinking class man,"* he always said, quoting some dead guy called Oscar Wilde. *"Not too many plumbers can quote Oscar Wilde,"* he'd brag. And each time he did he held up a beer, toasting himself. When he heard me rest my bike against the shed he looked up.

'Where's Mum?' I asked. We never said *"hi"* or *"how's it going."* Our conversations out in the garage normally started with me asking, *"where's Mum,"* leading him straight into a fresh, smartarse answer. He loved it.

'Inside working out what me and you aren't allowed to eat next week,' he said, laughing.

He called me his sounding board, (whatever the hell that was.) Lately Mum's dinner table talk was all about the latest fad diet. She'd bang on about fruits and veggies that were good and bad for you, and then she'd ruin it all with fish and chips on Friday nights, and sometimes the odd chicken parmy at the pub on Saturday nights.

He sucked on his beer. 'Remember last night's crap. As if potatoes or avocados can be bad for you.'

'I hear ya.'

'The people who fill those mags are a bunch of over-educated wankers who gotta sell fresh bullshit to us plebs week in week out. Over-education's going to become a problem in this world before long, let me tell you. Then you know what'll happen?'

'Yeah what?'

'Be classified a disease like everything else. Then the over-educated will start educating the under-educated on how not to become over-educated like them. Be running courses before ya know it. Don't wanna end up like me, they'll say.' He sort of said that last bit in a dopey moose voice like Bullwinkle off The Rocky and Bullwinkle Show.

I cracked up laughing. 'You're an idiot, Dad. It's your fault. You bought that magazine for her on the way home, Saturday morning, remember?'

Now he burst out laughing. 'That's why I put up with listening to her. Gotta get my money's worth out of those pages.'

Mum was always going on about religion and food and Dad didn't really care that much for any of it, and he told me so whenever we were out of earshot. But he was an expert at keeping the peace. At the dinner table he never argued, only winked at Tommy and me while we ate what we were given and swallowed the crap. Not that Dad's a pussy or anything. He told me in private he was proud I'd stood up for myself on the bus, like he'd always taught me. I also knew the real reason why he always brought her magazines and chocolates, even flowers on Saturday mornings. So he could go to the pub to watch the races in the afternoon.

'Mum's worried about you.'

'Been talking to Mr. Debono, went fishing too.' I held up the trout.

'Nice.' He drained his beer, and then his expression fell into a frown. 'You haven't been fishing with that Old Nick guy, I hope.'

Bang. He knew straight away. My face must have betrayed me. He didn't even wait for my reply and the truth was, I didn't really have one. I hadn't shown much interest in fishing before. Dad's a workmate and a dad rolled into one and when we worked together, he'd tell me crazy stories of what he got up to when he was younger and I found it hard to lie to him. 'I went to a place Nick showed me … he just happened to be there today, too.'

He gave a wearied look like he knew I was bullshitting. 'We agreed, remember.'

'Yeah, I know.'

Dad sighed. 'Listen. I know he's never caused any trouble, but you got plenty to do with your mates over the holidays. If you wanna go fishing, take your mates next time and don't go near his camp, like we agreed. Guy just wants to be left alone in peace.'

That wasn't true, otherwise Nick would tell me not to come around at all. 'Will you tell her?'

He tightened his lips in thought, then said, 'No, but don't forget you put me in the shit too. I'm the one that's s'posed to kick your arse and you're getting too old for that.' His eyes lit up. 'Boy. The sacrifices I make for you. Remember when she dragged me to church for six months in your final year of primary school. Gave up every freakin' Sunday morning, just so they'd think I was making an effort to convert so you had a better chance at getting into that mick school. Now I'm still covering your arse for shit like this.'

We both laughed at the memory. Dad had looked like a bulldog chewing on a wasp each time he walked through those church doors, then I laughed even harder and said, 'You'll have to do it all again for Tommy next year.'

'Pig's arse. Not doing that again. Hey, we can go fishing, you and me and Tommy, tomorrow after work.'

Hopes rose within me, then I realised the difficulty of getting him out of the pub where – as Mum was always willing to point out – he was as regular as the light fixtures on Saturdays. Even still, I said, 'Okay then, you're on.' But I wouldn't tell Tommy because I didn't want him being let down too.

He cracked another beer. 'Take that fish inside, I'll gut it for you.'

'No probs.' I wandered inside feeling bad for him too. I'd let him down and he was still going to cover for me, so I made the decision to do the right thing by Dad and not go back to Nick's.

CHAPTER 5

Dad and I had to finish off laying a drain the next morning before he went to the pub. He didn't mention fishing once. I did the right thing in the arvo and chose not to go to see Old Nick. (In my mind I'd already broken the promise I'd made to myself the night before. I'd be back out there as soon as I could.) By the time I fixed the tyres on my pushy it was getting too late anyway so instead, I played cricket in the street with Tommy and his mates between rain showers. Normally I'd ride down to the pinnies and hang out, but there was a good chance I'd bump into Debono down there and I was also saving my money for a new ten-speed racing bike.

After being dragged along to church on Sunday morning, I headed straight out to Roddy's house on the other side of town where I kept my motorbike. Together with Cudgy, we rode through the back streets and the bush tracks to the abandoned quarry, about four kilometres out of town where we met Meatlips and Soupy.

Before each race we held a meeting in our clubhouse, built up a tree years earlier by the Botwin brothers, four of the town's champion footballers and mad bluers. Dad was mates with them and they all drank together in the pub. Bruce, the oldest Botwin used to be the town's footy captain until the youngest brother, Loopy Lenny shot him in the ankle down in that very same quarry. Each time I climbed the ladder up to the clubhouse, I was reminded of the story Dad had told me many times.

When Dad was about eighteen, he and the Botwins went on one of their many wild pig hunting trips past Hay, in the outback of New South Wales. They came up with the bright idea to tie a few live ones up and bring them back to let loose in the quarry, so they didn't have to travel all that way again. They used the tree house so they could shoot at the pigs from a safe spot. Only problem was the pigs wouldn't come out from the bushes while they were there, so one day Lenny went down to scatter them out. The second eldest Botwin, Frankie let a shot off while Lenny was in the bushes and he didn't appreciate it too much and fired back. Bruce was climbing down the ladder at the time and Lenny, thinking Bruce was the shooter, thought he'd teach his older brother a lesson and fired into the bottom of the ladder. It was a poor shot, shattering the ankle and ending one of the town's great footy careers.

I was in the pub one day with Dad – he was drinking with Lenny – when I told them how we'd taken over the old tree house. Lenny explained how, as kids they'd managed to build it up in the trunk of a three-forked gum tree. First they lashed half cut truck tyres onto the branches with heavy rope and winched it up tight. Then they tied up treated pine logs – stolen from a park border in the middle of town – and tightened it all up again and built the tree house on top of the poles like a raft. Their theory was it would move as the tree grew and it seemed to work. It outlasted all types of weather over the years.

Up in the clubhouse, I sat next to Roddy and when he took his lumber jacket off, I reminded myself not to do so in the future because he reeked. The five of us owned these stylish lumber jackets, checker patterned in all different colours and lined on the inside with lambs wool. Most kids in Bushmore owned one but they were mainly worn in winter or to the pinnies at night, definitely not when we raced motorbikes. Roddy was rarely seen without his.

While the rest of us wore tee shirts with our club denim jackets over the top (arms cut off, of course), Roddy always wore his denim jacket under his lumber jacket. He'd been fat ever since kindergarten and was well aware of his tang as spring days warmed. Normally he drowned himself in Brut or Old Spice, sometimes both. He was always broke cause that's where his money went. Today, he'd either forgotten or it had worn off. But earlier, I noticed his pimples looked like fresh red-tipped volcano craters and I knew he'd spent the morning squeezing them, probably shooting pus at the mirror. He'd also begun to shave, must've been like a minefield for him. One splash of Old Spice on that face and he'd be on fire, screaming like a bitch. I laughed inside at the thought. He sipped his coke and turned to me. 'Told your old lady to get fucked yet, Gillings?'

I glared at him. This was a toughness issue with Roddy. In front of the others he continually asked me if I'd worked up the guts to tell my mum to get fucked. It was like a mental badge for him. Why did I have to go through this again? 'Of course not, you pus-rat. I told you—'

'Get round to it. I tell my old lady where to go every day, even this morning.' Roddy's dad had died when we were in grade two and his mum was an alcoholic.

I pictured the disgust on my mum's face if I ever dared to speak like that to her, microseconds before the cracking backhander. One time after school, she drove past and beeped her horn while I rode my pushy down to the shops. I put my thumb up like Fonzy from Happy Days would, and got the surprise of my life when I got home and she belted me across the earhole. In her speak, sticking a thumb up meant *"up your butt"* instead of *"aaayyy cool"*, the way The Fonze, and I meant it to be. She would kick my arse into next week if I ever dared to tell her where to go. Plus, I loved my mum. She was good to me and well, besides, Dad would dig out his thickest belt, fold in in half and strap my arse black and blue for saying anything like that to my mum. Other than at school, I hadn't been strapped for years and never wanted it again.

'Everyone else does it,' Roddy said.

'Couldn't give a rats arse,' I replied.

'Just do it, Gillo … get it over and done with,' Soupy said. I had no doubt Soupy would say it to his mum in a jiffy. He had the coolest mullet, spikey on top and cut half down the ears with the back trimmed square and dead straight across his shoulders. He also had four sleepers in his left ear. The other guys all had an earring each, but not me. Dad called me a fagg once for ordering a vegetarian focaccia at smoko. Imagine if I got an earring. Soupy wore a new set of tan leather cowboy boots, square at the toes. I wanted a pair, but the ten-speed racer had to come first. Last time I was at his house he showed me a scrapbook full of tattoos he'd planned to get once he left school and started working fulltime with his dad as a builder. I couldn't help but wonder where he was going to fit tattoos on those perfectly round, scrawny arms. Like soup bones, his older brothers reckoned. Hence the nickname.

Meatlips claimed to have said it to his mum once or twice; his dad was such a pussy. Worked at the post office. Meatlips often bragged he could beat his dad up if he tried. His nickname came from the birthmark spread over the right side of his lips and his cheek. I can't remember when we started calling him Meatlips – maybe sometime in early primary school. It never bothered him one bit and there was definitely no malice intended. Most people in town didn't even know his real name.

Then there was Cudgy with his dorky, freckled Ritchie Cunningham looks. His stepmum was a heifer cow, a smoke always hanging from her thick, red lips. When I thought of her, I saw lipstick stains on a hundred butts in the ashtray on the kitchen table. She'd beat him like the red-headed stepchild he was, or tell to him fuck off back, light a smoke, *then* make an ink spot out of him. Cudgy – or Captain Spineless as I often called him – offered no advice as usual. He sat in silence with his back against the wall, where Soupy had drawn the club's logo of a fist smashing through a globe of the world. Around the globe was our motto, *"RIDE THE WORLD"* scribbled above a list of ten rules – our club charter as Meatlips called it. Apparently real bikers called their list of rules a charter and we had to look like the real deal.

As for Roddy, I was fast beginning to tire of him, he was a constant downer on most things. Pus-filled pimples were taking over his head. The club was the only thing keeping our strung-out friendship going. I should've dropped him off years ago. Sometimes you get sick of your mates and I didn't like where Roddy was heading. He'd only begun to call me by my full last name of late, unless he wanted something or needed me to side with him. Then it was *Gillo* this or *Gillo* that, sometimes even *Jack,* like we were best friends again.

Unfortunately, I needed Roddy to keep my bike in his shed. Mum wouldn't even let me have a skateboard, let alone a motorbike. Dad was okay with it. He said if my mates have bikes, I should have my own and learn to ride properly, but Mum's word was final. I'm allowed to go to the quarry, just not allowed to ride. Why else would I want to go to an abandoned quarry … to hunt pigs?

Mum didn't really approve of these guys. She never said much about it, but I got the gist. Soupy moved into town in grade six and to stop me hanging around with him, she started making me go along to Father Frost's youth group, held on Friday nights in the hall behind the church for the Catholic kids in the town. It was the only place I was allowed to go to for a while back then.

Meatlips kept the book on our racing results for the inaugural title of The Bushmore Motocross Club Champion of The Year, or **T.B.M.C.C.T.Y.** for short. I was looking forward to the honour of winning it. I'd won six of the ten races so far and finished second in the others and was well in front with only five to go. Soupy had won four races, including the last two and was runner up to me four times, but he had two D.N.A's (Did Not Attend) beside his name.

As always, before each race we had a club meeting, chaired by Meatlips, the president. Our only item for debate was Debono. He'd asked if he could race.

'He's got no jacket.' I counted off each point on my fingers, citing rules 4, 8 and 10. 'He's too old and he's got a 125cc bike. They're the rules.'

Rule 4: All members must own and wear a LEVI denim jacket displaying the Club's logo and motto at all official meetings and club races. Jackets are not allowed to be washed.

Rule 8: A race competitor must be a current member of the Club and own a motorbike of no more than 80cc in power.

Rule 10: The club does not permit the voting in of new members older than the oldest of the original founders.

Meatlips was the oldest amongst us. Debono was several months older than him.

'Rule 10's especially for that jerkoff,' I said. 'Remember … we knew he'd suck up and try and race and the minute the shit hits the fan you start baggin' me out … like it's all my fault. Come on guys, get real. Next he'll wanna join the club, but you can tell him from me he can go fuck himself and plus … you have broken our second rule.' I read out aloud.

'Rule 2. No member may speak to outsiders of any motion put forward to, and voted on by the club and no member is allowed to invite outsiders to the clubhouse for any reason. Outsiders caught in the clubhouse will be bashed.

'You guys totally suck. Our racing schedule was voted on as a motion and you can't tell him when we're racing. That's the God damn rule. You guys just break fuckin' rules piss easy when you like.'

'Reckon you're taking it a little seriously, Gillo,' Soupy said, 'and plus he's been okay lately.' Soupy and Roddy had been knocking around with Debono in the first week of the holidays. Soupy also did an early morning paper run and I knew he pinched hardcore Swedish stick mags from the Newsagency and sold them to Debono.

'*Okay!* You reckon. He belted me on the bus, fuckwit.'

'More like you belted him,' Soupy said, grinning.

I grinned too. 'That was choice, should've seen him shit himself.'

'Yeah see, Gillo,' Cudgy said. 'You got payback. Bet he's over it, anyway.'

'Bet he's not. So we just change the rules, huh, cause you guys are crawlin' up his arse now. That two faced low life 'll shit on you as quick as look at ya.' I turned to Meatlips for support, but got none.

'We got no choice if he lobs, Gillo,' Meatlips said. 'We don't own the quarry, you know.'

'I know that, ya fuckin' retard.'

'Gillo,' Meatlips snapped, 'don't speak to the president like that, especially in a meeting.'

I glared at him. You're just another kid like me arsehole, I wanted to say, but held my tongue. 'So much for rules, huh.'

Meatlips was big on loyalty to the club (when it suited him). At the very first meeting – when he showed us the draft of the club rules – he expressed with intent that above all else, loyalty, discipline and obeying the club charter at all costs would carry the club through anything our teenage years might dish up, until we were old enough to get licenses and Harleys. He often said if we're really going to live up to our motto and *"ride the world",* then we had to learn that those three things must come before anything. Meatlips was the first of us to turn fifteen. The club was his idea and when we cast our very first votes, we elected him president and Meatlips said he wanted Roddy as vice president. None of us others really cared, but Roddy was stoked.

'We try and stop Debono,' Roddy said, 'he's just gonna become a bigger arsehole and we won't get our races done. Let's give him a penalty ... make him start back at the gate.'

'You always gotta win, Gillo,' Cudgy said. He and Roddy had been pretty thick too, lately. They'd pinched Roddy's mum's car twice in the first week of the holidays and gone bush bashing through the forest while she worked at the checkout.

'Just pointing out … that's why we got rules.' I couldn't believe they were ganging up on me like this.

'He's not even in the club and can't win nothing, so quit ya bitchin' Gillo,' Soupy said with his jaw slopping about. He was always chewing chewy.

'I know that, but don't think if you ever get chummy enough with him, he'll be able to join this club. Cause he won't. Rule 3, arsehole.'

Rule 3: All new members must be voted in unanimously by, and in the presence of all five original founders.

'*That* will happen over my dead body.' I gave Soupy a grin he could not return.

'Cut it yous guys,' Meatlips said and raised the gavel to end the meeting. He called it a gavel, but it was really just an old homemade, weighty mash hammer I'd knocked off from Dad's ute.

'Who votes to let him race if he lobs?'

Four hands rose, eight eyes fell on me.

'Tough shit, Gillo. Everyone have a fair race,' Meatlips said and slammed the hammer down on the floorboards, ending the meeting. The clubhouse shook.

'Ease up, fuck ya,' I said. 'You're gonna put that thing through the floor one day.' The floor was only made of timber off packing crates. I reckoned those cushioning tyres beneath us was the only reason we didn't go crashing through the bottom sometimes.

I wasn't happy, but I had to go with the flow at meetings because I had a skeleton in my closet. When we formed the club, I told Mum I needed a denim jacket and stressed it had to be a LEVI. It was all part of Meatlips' real deal thing. "*If you can't play football, at least dress like a footballer*", my dad always said and Meatlips wanted us looking like bikers.

So, what did Mum do, she bought me a LEE jacket from the Salvo's instead. *"A denim jacket's a denim jacket",* she had said. I was horrified. Not acceptable. And I didn't want to fork out my own hard-earned on an original LEVI. I was going to cut the arms off and write on the back anyway, so I sliced off the LEE tags without ruining the stitching. The only problem left was to figure out where I'd get a LEVI tag from. Dad would notice if I tagged a pair of his jeans. He treasured his old LEVI's and always wore them at the pub, so I visited my uncle Laurie over on Garden St. He was smoking pot with a few of his mates and none of them noticed when I snuck into his room and ripped the tag off a pair of jeans on the floor. Mrs. Debono did all of Mum's sewing and without thinking it through properly, I asked her to sew it on to my jacket. Now I was paranoid that if she told her son and he happened to climb the ladder and read our rules, he wouldn't hesitate to tell the others I had a LEE jacket to get me thrown out on my arse. As luck would have it though, she obviously hadn't told him and none of those idiots realised the design was slightly different to theirs. But I always felt like they'd find out one day, and they did.

'Don't panic, dude,' Soupy said. 'Here yar—' He passed some smokes around and lit up his own. Rule 9 said there was no smoking through meetings. (Meatlips didn't smoke)

Roddy and Cudgy lit up too. I slipped mine in my top pocket for later. Sure, I wanted to be part of the gang but didn't want to have a full ciggi before the race. Smoking made me feel dizzy, and I reckoned that's how Soupy nipped the edge off my riding in the last two races. He passed me the lighter.

'Waitin' till after the race,' I said, 'you're not getting my arse this time.'

He pumped out smoke rings. He's the only one amongst us who'd learnt to click his jaw. 'Where you been anyway, hardly seen you these holidays?'

'Working with Dad.'

'Not what I hear.'

'Been hanging with Old Nick too, guess you know that.'

'How'd you know he's not some weirdo, like those faggs that run your school?' Cudgy said.

'You ever heard he's a weirdo?'

Cudgy twisted his face and blew a trail of smoke from his nostrils. 'Guess not.'

'Then shut the fuck up … give ya a smack in the gob if you don't look out.'

'Just saying.'

'Yeah, well *just saying's* gonna get ya head smashed in if you don't shut it. Fucking spineless piece of shit.' I had never hit Cudgy before, but I didn't like what he said.

'Pair of bitches yous two,' Meatlips said.

'Yeah yeah, talk to cockhead … I didn't start it.'

Soupy passed me his smoke. 'Settle down mister fuckin' hypo. Take a drag.'

I dragged without drawing back, still I got that bitter taste of yesterday only tobacco could bring and handed it back.

'Fuckin' wuss,' Soupy said.

'No draw back, no head rush and you can watch my arse in the race.'

'Yeah, we'll see, Gillo.'

'Give me some chewy.'

'Buy your own, fuckin' tightass.' But he was already reaching into his pocket.

'Only have em' round you … cause you smoke.'

'Gillo wouldn't shout if his balls were wiped with Dencorub,' Roddy said and we all pissed ourselves laughing as we climbed down the ladder, ready to race.

Soupy was my only real danger. Roddy had the fastest bike, but he was too fat. The only thing he'd ever win was a pus squeezing distance comp. Cudgy simply didn't have the balls to take anything close to a racing line around corners and

Meatlips had an older bike, a clapped out Yamaha YZ. It needed a lot of work, probably a total re-bore.

As I was slipping on my helmet, I heard another bike over the far side of the quarry. Debono.

I hoped we could start the race before he realised we were over here, but then – like he could read my mind – he started riding over. Showing off and popping a mono as he got near us.

Race number eleven began, three laps of the rim of the quarry. After a brief discussion – which I chose not to be part of – Debono started back at the gate. I hammered my way to the front and took the first bend with Meatlips right behind me. He was soon replaced by Soupy who sat on my back wheel for the first two laps. No sign of Debono yet. On the third last bend I heard him coming up. He got inside Soupy and tried to come up the inside of me, but I shut him down before the corner by going as close as I dared to the edge of the quarry, almost skinning my left knee on the dirt. I knew he wouldn't try to take a real hard inside line, I'd cut him off and he'd either have to back off or I'd put him in the drink. The quarry's rock wall was a sheer drop and the lime green water below was supposed to be deep. No one had ever gone over the edge. Debono backed off and tried to take the inside line again when we straightened up, but I closed him down again, forcing him up the outside. He didn't come at me until the last bend, like he was toying with me. He could get past at any moment but I sensed something more sinister. I saw him coming up the outside of my back wheel, way too close. I slammed the throttle down and let my back wheel slide out so it clipped his front wheel. I held my line, let the wheel slide a touch more and heard his bike rev loudly. He tried to straighten, lost control and stacked into a clump of bushes. I glanced behind, laughing as I heard the high-pitched revving of another bike on my left. Soupy took me on the inside and straightened up for the finish line. I flattened my throttle but he had a bike length and speed and fist pumped his way over the line. I was spewing buckets.

Despite my anger, I was also excited because it was the best of our races so far and Debono had stacked. Soupy pulled off a mega move and I was stoked for him. (I also knew it would never happen again.) We high fived and cracked up laughing, watching as Debono pulled his bike from the bushes. 'That was fuckin' choice. Good race mate,' I said.

'Whooo hoooo,' Soupy yelled then pumped his fist in Debono's direction. Meatlips, Roddy and Cudgy finished in that order. Debono came flying up, full throttle, then skidded and dropped his bike right in front of me.

'Fuck you, Gillings.' He ripped off his helmet and threw it at me. I ducked and raised my arm, deflecting it over the edge. We heard it bounce off the rock wall and down into the green slime. I laughed at him; we all did, but Debono's mouth was wide open.

'Fuckin' arsehole. I'm gonna get you … you meant that.'

'You bet I did.' I jumped off my bike, ready, but left my helmet on in case he tried to punch me.

He sniffed and buckled his lips, eyes narrowed to slits. 'Take your helmet off, ya gutless fucking wonder.'

Meatlips stood between us and put his hands on Debono's chest. They were both the same sized kids. 'Hey, hey, it's all fair, all in the race. You had heaps of room, Debono.'

'Out of my way,' Debono spat.

Then Soupy also stepped in close, chin raised. 'Leave him alone arsehole, you're lucky we even let you race.'

Debono turned to Roddy. 'You gonna let these wankers get away with this?'

I stared at Roddy, not knowing what he'd do.

He lifted his helmet off and gave his tired, squinty look. 'Just a race man. Come on, Meatlips is right. You could've taken him on the outside, piss easy.'

'Debono,' Meatlips said, 'you stacked cause it's your fault … don't like it then fuck off. You're not part of this club anyway.'

Debono glared at Meatlips. Meatlips eyeballed him back. 'Anything happens to the clubhouse, we'll be looking for you and there'll be more than that helmet going over the edge. We'll toss you and your heap of shit bike in too.'

I think I grew a foot taller listening to Meatlips. I remembered his speeches of loyalty and discipline and he was sticking to all of his principles now, staring Debono down. I was glad he was our president and the club became stronger at that moment.

'See you on the bus, cocksucker,' Debono said to me.

'Yeah.' Meatlips raised his chin even more. 'Touch him and the next time you set foot in this quarry, all five of us will beat the living shit out you. I promise.'

Debono gave that livid, twisted scowl, picked up his bike and took off, flicking up stones and dust.

'Ride the world,' Meatlips said, holding up his fist toward Debono.

'Ride the world,' we all yelled, raising our fists like the two black American runners who gave the famous black power salute on TV at the Olympics back in the late sixties. Dad had told me all about the Aussie runner who finished second in that race and we felt every bit as powerful. I'd forgotten all about losing. We were thick. United in strength. A real club.

CHAPTER 6

We raced again the following day at the quarry. I won and Debono stayed over the far side, riding the jumps on his own. After the race we rode over and he left straight away. Guess he didn't want to talk to us. I went home that night, tired as all hell and got to sleep early, ready to be at Old Nick's by seven a.m. and determined to make the most of the last week of the holidays. Excited about going fishing, I rose at half five, ate two breakfasts and took some eggs from the chook pen for Old Nick. I told Mum I was going fishing with Meatlips and Soupy. I'd already worded them up, knowing they'd have my back if I needed it. I left with Rex, feeling alive and adventurous. These were fast becoming the best school holidays ever and this time, I wheeled my bike further into the forest and covered it with branches.

No smoke came from Nick's flue. I checked my watch. Seven o'clock, right on time. Disappointed, I didn't know what to do. I couldn't go near the camp if there wasn't any smoke. A noise startled me from behind, Rex barked and I nearly jumped out of my skin.

'Morning, young Jack.'

'Jees Nick, you been following me?'

'Had to check no one followed you, mate.'

'It was another kid from town, I made sure this time.'

'Good boy.'

I gave him the eggs.

'Thank you Jack, that's very thoughtful.'

I was glad he didn't say not to bring him anything because I liked giving him food. He stared at my fishing rod with his hands on his hips. 'Won't need that today.'

'Aren't we going fishing?'

'Surf fishing.'

'Choice.' That got me even more excited, but the ocean was miles away, probably a half-day's walk or more. 'How we gonna get there?'

He slapped me on the shoulder. 'I'll show you.'

Old Nick walked fast and we covered miles of forest. I had no idea of where we were other than knowing we were heading east where the bush thinned out and became dryer. Unlike the deep green forest surrounding his camp. He knew every track, every valley, every stream and where to cross. Finally we came out onto a gravel road guarded on either side by more thick bush. I could see run-down, rusty wire fences running parallel with the road and figured there were private properties. Then I saw a letterbox, and soon after, another.

'Where are we?'

'Turnbull Track. You know it?'

'Yeah.' A lot of four-wheel drive trails led off the Turnbull Track. We were deep in the heart of the forest.

After walking a long way further up a hill, he told me to sit, pointing to a log.

'Wait here. Don't move.'

And off he went down the road and out of sight around a bend.

I waited for half an hour until a red Holden station wagon approached. It skidded up beside me, forcing me to shield my eyes from the dust. A surfboard was strapped to the roof with an ocean-blue coloured fin facing sky high.

'Jump in,' he called through the open window. I didn't want to ask if we were stealing a car. Tossed in the back were fishing rods, a car fridge, fishing nets and buckets amongst other items.

I didn't know whether to get in or not.

'It's my car,' he said. 'I own it. Let's go.'

'Cool,' I said and tapped the top of the door. Rex leapt through the open window and sat beside Old Nick, who burst out laughing and ruffled the dog's coat. On the drive to the coast I asked him where he kept the car.

'That's another thing you don't need to know,' he replied in his cheery kind of way. I assumed there must be a property, maybe even a house at the end of the road. We drove towards the coast and found a quiet spot along the Great Ocean Road where we climbed down a rocky bank to the beach. He set the rods up using the cracks in the rocks for rod holders. With a bait pump, he sucked one-armed bandits from the sand. (I knew them as Bass Yabbies, they only had one claw.) He baited the two smaller rods. Nothing seemed hard or too much trouble for Nick, he went about everything with a smile, teaching me as he went. He was so organised, even hung a burley bucket off the rocks, twenty metres to our right with frozen scraps in it and explained how the current would work the burley down toward us and bring the fish around. He showed me what a cast net was and taught me how to hold it and stack the sinkers at the bottom of the net in my left hand. Then he taught me to cast the net wide into the shallows when I saw a school of small fish. Each time I pulled the net in it was teaming with live bait. We baited the surf rods and I learnt how to hook the livies (as he called them) through the tail carefully so they'd still be alive and could swim around, dragging the hook. Then he'd cast out as far as he could.

He left me in charge of the rods, changed into his wetsuit and paddled out on his surfboard to a wave breaking further out from the rocks. I'd not paid too much attention to surfing before, except when Mum and Dad took Tommy and I to the beach. Watching Old Nick surf wave after wave helped me see how it was done. He carved the long board through the face of the waves, legs bent and crouched, balancing with arms out wide like a seagull's wings. The white part of the wave never caught up with him and he skilfully stayed well clear of the rocks. He'd been out there for over an hour when a reel screamed. One of the smaller rods bent like crazy. Excitement swept through my body right to my fingertips as I reeled in a long silver fish. He fought like crazy and when I landed him, Nick paddled in.

'What is it?' I asked.

'King George Whiting. Good eating. Got him on a one arm bandit, huh.'

'Awesome.' King George, I thought. Sounds like I caught a good royal fish, longer than my forearm. I baited the hook again and couldn't wait to get the line back in off the rocks. As I cast out, the other small rod took off and Nick reeled in another one. We caught six more, one after the other. It was the most exciting fishing I'd ever done and then as quickly as they came on, the fish went off the bite.

'Got 'em on the first hour of the incoming tide,' he said. 'Remember that.'

Nick surfed some more while I caught a big flathead. Then he came in and skin-dived around the wall of the reef. I followed him as close as I could to the edge of the sharp, brown rock plateau stretching out from the beach. I had to stand three, four, even five metres back and sometimes more to dodge the spray off the bigger set waves. Nick was bobbing around off the wall in deeper water, when he shot his hand up and waved me over. His other arm was below the water and I think he must have been hanging onto a rock just beneath the surface. Otherwise the waves would have pummelled him into the wall.

I got as close as I could. Each set wave got bigger and rolled and thumped and boomed gently onto the reef. Spray hissed in the air, soaking my shirt and pushing me further and further back through fear of being washed off. I'd seen the news stories of fishermen being swept out and drowned at sea, but I felt safe with Nick in the water ready to catch me. 'Go back to the car,' he yelled, and ducked under a wave and came back up. 'Beneath the seat is a spray bottle full of detergent. Bring it here.' And under he went again.

I ran over the slab of reef. My feet were becoming accustomed to the sharp edges and I leapt over the pools the incoming waves had filled in. I found the detergent under the seat and returned, fast as I could. By this time he was sitting up on the edge of the reef in the same spot.

He grabbed the detergent bottle and grinned. 'Watch this.' He dived in off the rocks and under he went, and then he came back up. After repeating this several times, he surfaced holding a big crayfish in one hand, the bottle in the other. 'Got the sucker,' he called out. Between the waves he passed the cray to me and swam and dived along the rocks for a way, until he found another spot and down he went. Another crayfish, straight away this time. He dived around for a while longer and jumped out, wiping his long, wet hair back and beaming a grin.

'Ever tried crayfish?'

'Nope.'

'Can't say that tomorrow, son.'

I smiled, thinking we're going to eat them soon. It would have been nice to take one home for Mum. She'd be ecstatic, but at the same time would ask how I managed to catch crayfish. 'What's with the detergent?'

'Old Maori trick. Had a New Zealand mate who told me once if they couldn't get the lobsters out of their hollows between the rocks, they would spray detergent in. Lobsters don't like it and come out. Tried it one day and it worked a charm.'

I shook my head, amazed someone could think of doing that, let alone try it and find out it actually worked. I'd never be able to figure something like that out and wondered how I would cope in my future. I was destined to work with my hands like Dad, and I also wanted to leave school ASAP. My other dilemma was I wanted to make money. Real money.

Enough to become a millionaire and own racehorses that would win the Melbourne cup, or build a fast enough yacht to win the Sydney to Hobart race. I used to think other people had done it, so could I. But I started to realise it wasn't possible for me because I wasn't going to be a doctor or a lawyer. I'm not even smart enough to work through issues like the crayfish situation. I could strip my motorbike down and put it back together with no left over bolts or nuts. I could lay storm water drains, even put septic tanks in with Dad's backhoe on my own, but I'd have to become smarter in my future world to make real money, or work like ten men. It was a light-bulb moment for me and I resented not having a piece of paper to write it all down.

Nick and I drove back into the forest and parked on the side of a dirt road, then walked to his shack. He boiled up a crayfish and cooked a whiting. Both tasted magnificent. 'What are you going to do with the second cray?' I asked.

'You want to take it home for your mum, don't you?'

'She'd love it.' I'd already thought of how to extend my lie. The plan was to tell her that Soupy's older brothers took us fishing off a beach, and I found the crayfish trapped by the dropping tide in one of the shallow rockpools on a reef. I didn't know if a cray could get caught by the tide, but if I didn't know how plausible it was or wasn't, she'd have no idea. Dad would be an issue though.

'Might come back in the next couple of days and see if we can get some more. I'm going to give this one to some friends.'

Friends? He'd never mentioned he had any other friends, and that sorted out my *lying* situation.

'Take three whiting home,' he said. 'I'm going to eat the flathead tonight and keep the rest of the fish in the freezer.'

The freezer again? I didn't know if he was kidding or not.

I was a bit pissed off. I thought we'd at least have gone halvies. On the flip side, I had one less lie to tell and Mum wouldn't know what she was missing out on. She'd be happy with the fish again. Christ, I figured I could even tell her I'd caught the whiting in the river, she wouldn't know the difference. Once again, running it past Dad would be the problem though, so I knew I'd have to at least tell her the truth about where it came from.

I was tired after a long day, but I'd have to go down the pinnies after tea and word Soupy up to make sure we didn't cross wires, in case my mum bumped into him in the street.

On the way home I had a full belly and plenty of time to make sure there weren't any holes in my story. Luckily, Dad played darts at the pub that night. He filled in for a mate so he wasn't home. I remembered my promise to Mr. Debono and went up there to ask if he wanted a fish. He gutted all three while I waited and thankfully his son wasn't home. He kept one and Mum cooked the other two whiting up for us. I went with the story about going to the coast with Soupy's brothers, only to be told I wasn't to go driving with them anymore. They were yahoos, she said. I couldn't do a thing right, or wrong sometimes.

CHAPTER 7

Debono didn't turn up for Thursday's race. I won and figured I couldn't lose the title even if I didn't turn up for the last three races.

Sunday arvo we were scheduled to race again. When I picked my bike up from Roddy's, he wasn't home and his motorbike was gone. I expected to see him down at the quarry but when I arrived only Meatlips, Cudgy and Soupy were there. We practiced on the jumps while waiting for Roddy, then decided to race without him because he didn't show up. We were beneath the clubhouse chatting when we heard Roddy's bike screaming up towards us. I recognised the sound of his engine, but when it got close I could tell Roddy wasn't riding it.

Jason, his younger brother lifted the helmet. 'Roddy's been beaten up pretty bad, you guys have gotta do something. Come on, follow me.'

'What's happened?' Meatlips asked, but I already knew and I suspect he did too.

'Debono got him. He was on his way down here riding through the bush. Kicked the shit out of him. Busted nose, black eye, fat lip. Got him good. He's at home on the couch. Mum's called the cops.'

'Let's get over there,' Meatlips said. We rode to Cudgy's joint and left the bikes there so we didn't get busted riding on the roads in case the cops were at Roddy's. We walked the remaining two blocks.

Roddy was laid out on the couch in a bad way. Bright red Mercurochrome stained the cuts over his elbows; his eyes and nose were swollen and bruised. His mum came in followed by his Uncle Dan. He was Roddy's dead father's brother. We all knew he'd been rooting Roddy's mum for a while but they tried to keep it secret. I didn't like him. He had these bodgie, home-job tatts on his forearms and a thin face, hollowed cheeks and a black moustache. Sometimes I wondered what we'd all look like in the future and when I looked at Dan, I saw the future Soupy. Dan always struck me as a man pissed off at the world. More so now.

'You boys don't need to be around,' he said. 'Just upset him—'

'I've had enough outa you,' Roddy's mum spat, giving him a cross look.

'They'll cause more trouble this lot—'

'Piss off will ya.' She pointed toward the door.

Dan gave us a filthy look then went back to the kitchen.

'Boys. Maybe you just say hello, then leave.'

'Can't we hang for a while, Mrs. Rodwell?' Meatlips said. 'We're gonna look out for him over this, don't you worry.'

'Brett, please.' She cast her eyes toward the kitchen. 'I don't want anyone else talking like that. The Police have gone over to the Debono's trying to sort this mess out.'

'We just wanna stay, only for a bit,' Meatlips said.

She sipped her beer in thought. 'For the time being, but don't stir him up, please boys. Don't want him going out to the shed, either.'

'Yes Mrs. Rodwell,' Soupy assured her. She disappeared into the kitchen. We heard raised voices as she ripped into Dan.

'Roddy, what the fuck happened?' Cudgy asked.

'Bastard took me out from behind, ran me off the track. I stacked and couldn't get the bike off my leg. He just started kicking the shit out of me. Had those Rossi boots on and all. Thought he was a mate.'

"Told you so," I wanted to say. I wasn't looking forward to facing Debono on the bus in the morning, first day back at

school. If he came at me, I'd have to go hard like last time. I longed for a set of Rossi motorbike boots. Debono's had a steel trim on the outside of the toes. He always left them on his back porch and I thought about sneaking up to his place that night to lob a turd in them as payback.

'He's never been a mate, Roddy. Arsehole's got a screw lose.' Meatlips shook his head, slowly. 'We're gonna tighten it up a little for him when we catch him.'

'Don't do nuthin' without me,' Roddy said. 'I wanna fuck him up big time.'

'We'll wait, don't worry.'

'Why'd they call the cops?' Soupy asked.

'Mum had to. Uncle Dan was trippin' out threatening to go over there himself.'

We stayed with Roddy all afternoon, most boring last afternoon of the holidays ever, watching repeats of Get Smart and Gilligan's Island. We'd always hung out in his shed where we'd work on our bikes, smoke fags and even gotten drunk out there on a couple of Saturday nights through the last term.

Mid-afternoon a car pulled up. I was surprised as I recognised Father Frost's large gold coloured Ford LTD. Roddy's family weren't Catholic. I'd been an altar boy once, lasted about four weeks before he booted me off for talking through Mass. He'd hardly spoken a word to me since that day.

The priest walked to the door and knocked, dressed in black with a white collar. He was tall but shaped like a bell, with a wide bulging gut, hunched back and stooping, rounded shoulders. He reminded me of Baby Huey from the old cartoons. Maybe it was his waddle from side to side as he walked, or the lips, always poised open a touch like a dead fish.

'Someone's here,' Jason called out. Dan appeared and answered the door. He looked Father Frost up and down.

'What do you want?'

Father Frost sighed and pulled his priestly smile from somewhere deep beyond those puffy, beetroot coloured cheeks. 'Excuse me, I want to talk to Mrs. Rodwell.'

'She don't need to talk to a priest. No-one's dead.'

'Listen, err Dan is it?' Father Frost had his hand extended. 'Gray … Graham Frost. Every one calls me Gray. So please, feel free. Surely we can talk this through.'

They shook hands and with those pacifying priestly words, Dan seemed to calm down a little.

Mrs. Rodwell appeared. 'Just show him in.'

The priest came through. He asked how Roddy was but I think he faked concern. Roddy said he'd be okay and Father ignored the rest of us, only giving me a passing glance from those sagging, bloodhound like eyes as he walked straight into the kitchen after Dan. He was an uncomfortable man to be around.

We heard voices. 'Go listen,' Meatlips said to me and I crept over to the sliding door, able to hear every word through the gap between the door and the wall.

'The Debono boy says Neil threw a rock at him first,' Father Frost said.

'That's fuckin' bullshit,' Dan replied.

'Don't swear,' Mrs. Rodwell warned him.

'I couldn't care less who he is. Neil wouldn't have done that.'

I put my hand over my mouth and sniggered. Roddy would have chucked a rock for sure at Debono, had he had half the chance.

'Whether or not it happened Mr. Rodwell, that's what Anthony told the police. I was present.'

Ever since we were altar boys, Father Frost was the only person I'd ever heard call Tony Debono by his full first name, Anthony. Debono had been his favourite back then. He and I were also okay at the time before he turned into such a prick.

'Lying little bastard.'

'Dan—'

'It's fine, Mrs. Rodwell,' Father said.

'That boy works for you, doesn't he?' Dan asked.

There was a pause. 'Mows the lawns, does a bit of gardening at the presbytery, yes.' Another pause. 'For pocket money. Anthony really is a kind boy, I'll admit a little misguided at times and he clearly has done the wrong thing here.'

Debono got all the jobs at the presbytery, that's how he could afford such a good motorbike.

'Why aren't the cops telling us this?' Dan said. 'Why you?'

'I'm sorry Mr. Rodwell. They had other business to attend so I offered to come over and see you myself. I know the family very well, his father has agreed to punish his boy for what he's done.'

'If I don't press charges,' Mrs. Rodwell said.

There was a long drawn out silence before the priest said, 'The police have agreed not to charge him, it's one boy's word against the other.'

'Ahhh ... jees,' Dan said, 'I know Tony senior too, he's a man of his word. S'pose I'll give him a buzz myself. Guess it's only a couple of kids punching on. We're just angry, that's all.'

'I understand. He intends to call you, Mrs. Rodwell. Shall I tell him he can ring tonight?'

'That will be okay, Father. Thank you for coming over,' Roddy's mum said.

I'd heard enough so I moved away. They talked for several more minutes and the priest slipped out the back door.

CHAPTER 8

Soupy fought like a cut cat, according Mitch Ladbroke who also worked an early morning paper round. Mitch caught my bus and reckoned he saw the whole fight. It was a week after Roddy's bashing and Soupy had just picked up his paper round at the rear of the newsagency. As he rode off down the dark alley sometime near five thirty a.m., Debono came from nowhere and threw a stick in his spokes and brought him down, then laid the boots in. Same as he did to Roddy, but Soupy got up. Despite being the width of an envelope, I knew he'd never give in and the fight spread over the fence into Mr. and Mrs. Wendsley's front yard. When Mr. Wendsley came out to see the ruckus, Soupy was bleeding from the nose and swinging a garden stake from the Wendsley's roses, threatening to kill Debono if he came near him again.

Debono got on the bus that morning and saw me sitting safely in a corner seat out of reach against the window. His smirk spread from ear to ear, without a care in the world that he didn't have any friends. I couldn't help thinking he'd kept true to his word because he hadn't laid a hand on me, yet. I knew my turn was coming. He was picking us off one by one and he had three to go, but there were roadblocks. Cudgy's older sister lived with Frankie Botwin and Cudgy was the type to go to Frankie, who was psycho enough to do something about it even if it meant belting up a kid. Debono was smart enough to know you didn't mess with the Botwins in Bushmore. Meatlips could handle Debono by himself, I had no doubt about that, meaning I was the obvious choice for next in line.

I knew Soupy and Roddy's bashings were my fault and slowly but surely I began spending more time with Old Nick and drifted away from my mates. I also started riding my pushy to school to avoid Debono. With no gears it was a hard slog up and down the hills on the Cape Road. I'd saved enough cash to buy my own ten-speed racer, but I had a suspicion Mum and Dad were going to buy me one for my upcoming birthday, so I decided to hold on to my cash and wait.

I lived my life wondering when my beating would come. After school was the most obvious time and I made sure I was with one of the other guys whenever I went to the pinnies. Rex was always by my side too and if Tommy and his mates wanted to play cricket, I mowed a pitch in the back yard so we didn't have to play in the street.

In the club we stuck together and rode on Sunday afternoons. Soupy and I won the remaining races and I took the title. We had a little ceremony where Soupy wrote across the shoulders of my jacket in texta,

IN. T.B.M.C.C.T.Y. 1982

(IN was short for inaugural.)

I only had the other four members to enjoy the moment with. I couldn't tell anyone else through fear of it getting back to Mum. Debono would ride on the other side of the quarry and piss off real quick when he saw us coming. Soupy was scheming up his revenge big-time and discussed ways of trapping him at the meetings. Meatlips didn't like any of them and would tell him to hang off, but I knew Soupy and Roddy were becoming very impatient.

On Saturdays when I didn't have to work, I went down to Old Nick's with eyes in the back of my head and Rex for company. He'd never bitten anyone but all dogs have the fight in them and he made me feel safe. Nick and I went to the coast often. At first he'd make me wait at the log while he got the car. Then one particular morning, I was surprised when we reached the log and he said, 'Follow me, son.'

We walked further along that deserted road, up the hill where it narrowed to a bush track beneath the reaching manna gums. There was no indication it was a driveway at all until I saw sun gleaming off the windows of a house up ahead through the bush. We went out the back to a shed. He found a key under some bricks and opened up the doors. The red Holden was inside with the surfboard already on the roof. A deep freezer box hummed away against the wall. I smiled to myself. Nick's mysterious freezer. Inside the shed he found another key and we wandered over to the house, painted brown with stained windows and a steep roof. Dad would've hated putting that roof on.

'Whose house is this?

'Friends of mine. Sometimes I sleep here through winter.' The house was clean inside with timber floors and walls, the furniture was better than ours. He made us coffee and toast with Vegemite, then showed me some tomatoes and other vegetables he'd planted in the backyard. Already, they looked a lot more mature than my father's. We crossed a lawn area beneath a row of pines, out of place amidst the gums. Black cockatoos shrieked and cracked their way through the pine nuts above our heads.

'Let's get a move on. Bad weather's coming.'

I saw only blue sky between the trees. 'How do you know?'

'The black cockatoos live high up in the rain forest. They only come down here to the east side when the heavy storms are about to come through.'

It made sense. I'd seen these birds many times. A whole flock of them would descend on Bushmore, wherever there were pine trees. They'd crack the pinecones open and eat the nuts in the centre, dropping the cones everywhere and destroying the parks and backyards in town. From now on though, I would always look on them as a warning rain was coming.

We went back to the shed and pulled some bait from the freezer, then loaded the wagon with the rods and his wetsuit.

'Jump in, we're off.' He turned the key. The car made a dying, cranking noise but wouldn't start. He tried again and again. 'Think the battery's on its last legs. Get out and push.'

The car rolled nicely on the dirt and picked up just enough speed down the slope for Nick to be able drop the clutch and kick it in the guts. The car started and off we went to the ocean.

Despite our friendship, I still thought of him as Old Nick and on calmer days he began to teach me how to surf. At first he'd swim out beside me and push me into the waves. I'd gotten the hang of standing up and going straight, but I'd have to jump off quick and grab the board before I hit the rocks. Turning and riding the face like Nick did was going to take a little longer, but he was patient. On this day though, I'd never seen the ocean angrier. A ground swell was running, bringing in waves taller than I ever imagined, as high as our church. Nick paddled so far out to sea I had to climb up the steps on the embankment beneath the road to see him. He surfed on his own for hours and wouldn't let me fish off the rocks, so I just sat and watched. Nick was right about the rain too. Dark clouds were building up over the Otways from the west.

Finally he came in, exhausted. He changed from his wetsuit and we sat up on the dry reef just staring at the ocean and eating sandwiches I'd brought from home. Those massive waves mesmerised us both. We must have been forty or fifty feet back and still copped tingles of ocean spray off the bigger sets.

'How come you moved to our side of the forest, Nick?'

'Too much crap going, mate. Greenies and loggers carrying on. Loggers wanted me out, thought I was a greenie, and the greenies wanted me to join their fight because the loggers were wrecking my home, so they said.'

'But they are, aren't they?'

'Not really, they're locals who've got families to feed. Most of the greenies come from Melbourne, anyway.'

'I thought you'd be on their side.'

'I'm not on anyone's side, came over here where I can do my own thing. Don't want any part of it. The Otways will become a battle ground soon, you watch.'

I knew a little about it from kids at school, some had fathers who were loggers. 'Who's right?' I asked.

'No one's ever a hundred per cent right, remember that son. Wherever you go, whoever you listen to, people will tell you they are right and give you their opinions until they are blue in the face. But opinion is neither right or wrong, it's just opinion based on their circumstances. I can only give you my opinion, based on what's right for me. I live in the forest so I need it. The loggers create a lot of noise and ruin the habitat of animals. They also mess the place up but the forest reclaims it and regrowth happens pretty quickly. Greenies all want homes to live in. Those homes are made of timber, wooden cupboards and furniture, all that stuff, yet they don't want a logging industry. Loggers need their jobs to support their families, but I guess without the greenies, loggers would strip the place bare. They've done that to plenty of other forests.'

It seemed fair to me. 'Why do you live here like this?' I expected him to tell me again there were things I didn't need to know, like last time, but he didn't. Instead, he turned and I saw the relaxed, peaceful look in his eyes.

Then he winced and said. 'I'm on the run.'

I sat upright. 'On the run? What from, the cops?'

Beneath those whiskers, I suddenly saw a different side to Nick. His eyes widened, brows lifted, stretching his weathered skin. 'Yeah. I assaulted two of 'em.'

'Why?'

'They came to arrest me. I can trust you to keep this to yourself, can't I?

'My oath. Never told anyone anything about you.'

He nodded. 'Good. I got drafted to Vietnam in 67.'

'Drafted?' I'd heard the term before and I knew it involved war because my uncle Laurie had been sent to Vietnam.

'I was twenty years old, they wanted me to go fight some war.'

'Drafted means you gotta go … no choice right?'

'According to their rules.'

'Why didn't you go?'

'I live by different rules. We all have sacrifices to make in life and leaving the people I loved and the place I lived in was one of them. The way I saw it, I'd have to leave anyway, but on their terms, not mine. To go off and fight for someone else's political agenda in a foreign land, that's just crap. After my father went through World War 2, he busted his gut to get to Australia for a better life, not to have me play the same game of soldiers and I agreed with him. Everything about it was crazy.'

I detected a slight anger in his voice.

'My father once told me, when the game's over, all the kings and queens and pawns get packed away in the same box. We all begin with a breath and die on a breath. It's the middle where our conscience comes into the equation and I can do my own thinking. You don't have to live on *their* terms and who the hell are *they* anyway. Bunch of politically minded wankers telling me I gotta go and get killed while they hide their own kids overseas and in universities, or in plum jobs or whatever to avoid the draft. I knew what was going on.

'It shouldn't make a difference who the hell you are, but it does. I wrote them a letter telling them that if the people drafting me wanted to send their sons to come and fight beside me, then I'd go. Sent the same letter to the papers and it got printed.'

'What happened?'

'Politicians don't appreciate being told what they should do either and they don't like being shamed, so they sent the cops after me. I couldn't live at home. They came to my mates' houses where I'd been staying. That caused problems too. A couple of those guys got dragged down the cop station. Back in those days telephone books had two purposes, looking up numbers and slamming you over the head if the coppers thought you were bullshitting.'

'Telephone books ... why?'

'Only leaves a mark on the inside, cops used to say. Rough times, mate. Lived on the Gold Coast. Know where that is?'

'Bottom part of Queensland, right?'

'That's it. The Goldy was a bit of a war zone itself at the time. Government and councils saw surfers as vermin. Tried to weed us out so the developers could move in. Didn't work though, it was our home. But try being a surfer *and* a draft dodger.

'Couldn't have nothing in my name, couldn't get a real job or rent a house. Couldn't pay Metaxas Metaxas.'

'What the hell are you on about?' I said, confused.

He laughed. 'Me taxes. Couldn't pay me taxes. My last name's Metaxas.' He spelt it out for me.

'Oh, I get you now.'

'My parents are Greek. That's how I know so much about herbs. Growing stuff with my dad over the years. Miss them a lot and call every now and again to let them know I'm okay.

'So I moved about, working for cash when I could find it. Slept where I could; factories, the floor of the surf club, anywhere. But friendships begin to wane fast when you start impacting too much on the lives of others. They don't mean it, but you begin to hear what they're not saying. I knew I had to move on and get out of Queensland.

'I was sleeping at the Currumbin Surf Club. Few of the older crew lagged me in and the cops blocked both exits early one morning. Only way out was through them. One officer got knocked out cold and they made a song and dance in the media. Now I'm a fugitive. They dropped the draft dodging charges years ago, but they don't forget about assaulting cops.

'Spent two months driving down the east coast until I found this place. It's got everything I need. Excellent waves, good fishing, and a huge forest where no one bothers me. No place in the country like it and I'm used to the cold water and the winters now.'

'Wouldn't it have been easier just to go?'

'And blow people up?'

'Beats living in a cold forest.'

'I think you underestimate war, son. You reckon dying in a hot jungle is better than living in a cold forest? This was my life, my everything, and other people were willing to put that in front of a machine gun. I don't want to be remembered as a hero. I want to *be*. Full stop. I don't have much here, but I have what those arseholes were willing to throw away. My life.'

'Okay, I get it. Now that you put it like that, I guess.'

'See, now you're thinking right. All I wanted to do was surf and work. Pay my way in life. I didn't want to get killed.'

I wondered if I'd do the same in that situation. 'Currumbin. That's where you're from, huh?'

'Born and bred. Great place back in the sixties. See that logo on the stick.'

'Stick?'

'The surfboard.'

'Yeah.' I had noticed the sticker of a barrelling blue and green striped wave with cockleshells and fruit.

'See the name beneath the logo, Michael Peterson. Best surfer in the world at the time. A paddling machine. Shaped that board for me. The Goldy was just a bunch of small towns back then, an exciting place to be. Warm water, friendly people. Then the money moved in and wrecked the joint.

'Here's different. I've made some great friends, you included.' He patted me on the shoulder. 'I'm glad I met you and people like Leon Jones and his wife Carrie. They own the house. Met Leon in the surf a few years ago. They're from Melbourne. I look after their house. Clean up a bit, mow lawns, that sort of thing. Gives me a bit of cash for petrol and a few supplies. I don't need much to get by. You'd be surprised how easy life can be when you simplify it.'

I thought of all my possessions, my mum's material possessions and all the stuff like having to go work every day and washing machines. All the different soaps and detergents and floor cleaners Mum had to buy, that probably just did the same job in the end anyway. Things Nick had little need for. As far as I knew, he washed his clothes and dishes in the Otway creeks. 'What do you miss the most?'

'Everything. Family, cousins, the surf club. Surfing with mates. All that. My girlfriend took up with one of my mates. Can't blame her, I guess.'

'Doesn't seem fair.'

He chuckled. 'You ever heard anyone tell you life's fair, son?'

I thought about it. 'No one's ever going to say that.'

'See. Words never before uttered.'

'What about TV? Don't you miss it?'

'Never a big watcher, mate.'

'Don't you want to know who shot J.R.?'

He laughed and ruffled my hair. 'Who's the hell's J.R.?'

'He's—'

'Spare me, son. Don't wanna know. There's better things to do than sitting around watching nothing.'

I thought about that too. When I visited him, telly was the last thing on my mind.

'No footy or cricket?'

'Used to drive past cricketers on my way to the surf. Days would be stinking hot and I'd think, stuff that. And I couldn't name any of your footy sides down here, either.'

'You can be an Essendon supporter then.'

'Who's Essendon?'

'What? It's my football side. You can't live in Victoria without having a footy side and we'll win the flag next year. Can feel it in my bones.'

'All right then.' He grinned. 'An Essendon supporter I am, just for you.'

He ruffled my hair again. I liked it when he did that. We talked some more and it was the best day I'd ever spent with Nick before we headed home beneath the teaming rain.

CHAPTER 9

When I arrived home that night Dad was working in the downpour, moving some of the woodpile into the garage to keep it dry. I was already soaked to the skin from the ride home and began to help. We stacked a couple of days worth against the wall under his cherished '78 and '79 Big M Girl calendars. 'Where's Mum?' I asked.

'Reading up on how to lose weight by eating more.'

I recalled how last night Mum had lectured us on some new *eat more – lose weight* diet she'd discovered in one of her mags.

'What a load of sheep shit that was,' he said.

We both laughed. I could tell he was drunk after a usual Saturday arvo at the pub. Moving the woodpile gave him an excuse to have a few more beers before dinner.

'Where you been? Just missed your mates. Meatlips and Roddy. They were with that other kid, the skinny little faggot with all the earrings.'

I panicked. 'Did they talk to Mum?'

'No, they just came to the garage.'

'Where'd they go?'

'Now how would I know that?' Dad was right, that was a stupid question.

'Just gave them a copy of your twenty-first photos, you know.'

'Better fuckin' not have,' I warned. He claimed to have these embarrassing photos of me asleep when I was young – sucking my thumb or playing with my nuts – that he was going to show everyone at my twenty-first. I honestly had no idea if he was serious or not because he never showed me the photos.

I went inside and changed into some dry clothes then rang Roddy. If they weren't at the pinnies, they'd be in his shed.

His mum answered. She called out at the top of her voice and after a minute or so, Roddy was on the line.

'Gillings, get your arse over here. We got a grouse plan to get Debono.'

I wasn't going over there in the rain. 'A plan?'

'Fuck yeah.'

Roddy's plans always meant trouble. Like the time two years ago when there was a New Year's Eve dance at the footy club. Roddy conned us into stripping the stink beans off the stink bomb tree near the oval. We scattered them on the dance floor at ten minutes before midnight while the Nut Bush was playing. The stink bombs got squashed and the smell cleaned the place out instantly, ruining New Year's Eve. We got our butts kicked for that one.

'I'll give it a miss, Roddy. Been a big day and it's pissing down.'

'Come on, it's Saturday night. Come over, have a few beers.'

'Nah, mate.' Alcohol went straight to my head. I tried to like it just to be in with the gang, but while the others were easily able to drink a half dozen cans each, I was what's known as two can screamer and by my fourth, I'd be throwing up.

'Total wuss, Gillings. Hey listen. See you later on tonight, anyway.'

'What?' I heard him laughing through the handset. 'What do you mean, later on?'

'Tonight, tosser. Just be awake.' And the line went dead.

I fell asleep while waiting sometime around nine, thinking he was full of crap as usual or they were going to roof rock Debono's house or something silly like that. Then a noise woke me. Someone was tapping on my window. I got up to take a look and saw Cudgy's face inside a hooded raincoat.

'Gillo, get up … get up.' He slurred his words through moist lips and a slack grin. I wanted to stay in my nice warm bed, but Cudgy urged me on and so I dressed and slipped my raincoat on, pulled my fly screen off and jumped through. Rex followed. Cudgy led me toward the front street where a car idled a few doors down, out the front of Debono's house.

The heavy rain was gone, leaving only a light drizzle and as we reached the gate, the car revved and inched forward, then jerked to a stop. I saw the rope. Roddy's mum's car reversed back up to Debono's fence then accelerated hard, tearing a full section of the timber fence out of the ground. The car came racing up the street towards us and skidded in the wet, the heads inside lurched forward. I recognised Roddy and Soupy in the front seat. Cudgy ran up and dived through the back window, headfirst.

I heard the cry of, 'Whooo hoooo,' as Roddy took off, fist pumping the air with the fence scraping and bounced along behind the car.

Soupy hung out the window waving his arms and yelling out, 'Didya like the plan, Gillo?' And they disappeared round the corner doing a burnout. Tyres screeched on the shiny bitumen and fence palings were flying end over end.

I stood in the street, alone, laughing in total disbelief.

'What the hell's happened?' my dad asked from beside me, wearing only his jocks.

'No idea.'

'What's going on out there?' Mum called.

In a low voice, Dad said, 'What are you laughing at and what the hell are you doing out here?'

Through my laughter I said, 'Someone totalled their fence. Just heard the noise like you and came out.'

'Yeah, well they called out your name. Sounded like that grotty mate of yours, the one with arms like pipe cleaners.'

Mum switched the porch light on and he shut up.

Debono's parents appeared and Dad went inside to get dressed. Mr. Debono held his two arms over his head beneath the streetlight staring back at what was left of his fence. The Morrisons next door came out, so too did half the street. They gathered beneath umbrellas, talking and pointing. Tony Debono stood beside his father, who was now scratching his head and staring both ways up and down the street, dumbfounded. Debono saw me. I waved and wandered inside up the drive, put my fly screen back on, dried myself off again and went to bed pissing myself laughing. Good old Roddy had one hell of a grouse plan.

CHAPTER 10

Dad didn't say a word regarding what he knew about the fence, and even went down with a couple of beers to help Mr. Debono repair it the following day. A week later my fifteenth birthday came and went in a flash. Mum, Dad and Tommy gave me a new watch and a portable tape recorder. It took only four 'D' size batteries, had a slide out handle in the top and was so small it fitted into my school bag. I was happy with the tape recorder but another watch made me disappointed. I'd dropped enough hints regarding the ten-speed racer and even told Tommy heaps of times to mention it to the oldies. Yet the damage wasn't all that bad. I got a total of fifty bucks off the relos. At least I didn't have to use all my own cash for the racer, which I bought the next day from the hardware shop. No more hard arse rides to school in the headwind. I now had gears.

Mum capped the party at eight kids. Four from school and the boys from the club. We had to get along with my two younger cousins from Melbourne, who I had nothing in common with. (Tommy disliked them too.) Dad and my uncle Laurie did the cooking and Mum and her sister haggled and fussed over the rest of the work. Soupy and the boys brought around a present, a slab of cans in an esky and stashed them down at the creek. We snuck away on dark after everyone left and hid down the bank drinking and toasting me, the last of our little group to turn fifteen.

It was a cold Friday evening, the wind howled down the gully. Soupy pulled out a rolled cigarette, much fatter than a tailor made. He lit up and took a few tokes and passed it to me.

I held it, watching the wind temper with the lit end. It smelt different, nice too. I knew it was a joint, still I asked what it was.

'It's a fuckstick, ya fuckstick,' he said and we all burst out laughing. 'A present for you ... it's good to have older brothers.'

Keen to explore new boundaries, I dragged on it and became instantly dizzy. I dropped the joint and reached out for the tree beside me. Meatlips picked it up, toked on it a few times and passed it around. My head spun, kind of like the time when I had my first cigarette, only a lot worse, or better. I didn't really know. When my turn came around again I was silly enough to take another few hits. After that I tried to finish my beer, but I didn't feel like drinking anymore, didn't feel like speaking either. Didn't feel like doing anything much at all really other than enjoy the moment, doing nothing, just laughing.

We arranged to ride on Sunday through the bush tracks down Denhams Creek near the quarry. All except for Meatlips, who had to attend his auntie's birthday. He said he'd find us at sometime in the afternoon, either at the quarry or the creek.

Ripping Debono's fence out of the ground was fun, but not enough payback to satisfy Soupy and Roddy. They were anxious to teach him a major physical lesson. I could see they were both pissed off at Meatlips who kept telling them to wait for the right opportunity. He hadn't been in the car on the night they ripped the fence out.

We met at the clubhouse. Soupy passed around the smokes.

'Nah mate,' I said.

'Given up?'

'Just not into it.' (I'd barely started.) I didn't like the taste and also, I'd taken a keen interest in Old Nick's fitness level required for surfing. Smoking wasn't going to let me get fit, plus I was afraid Soupy might ask me to chip in for the packet and I didn't want to waste my money.

'We got a mega plan to get Debono,' Roddy told me.

'Another plan? 'Fire away.'

'He'll be here later on. We wanna get him down into the bush and take him out on one of the tracks near Denhams Creek.'

'How you gonna do that?'

'You and Cudgy will do it. Think of some way to get him to follow you down towards the creek. We'll be waiting.'

'He's not even here,' I said.

'He will be. He's here every Sunday riding with Scott and Neville,' Soupy said.

'Scott and Neville?' I asked, thinking Debono had some new mates.

'Scott no mates and Neville will have.' Soupy almost burst out laughing before he finished speaking. We all joined in.

We rode the tracks for miles down through Denhams Creek. It had rained a lot and we had great fun churning mud up at each other. We checked the quarry about two o'clock, sure enough Debono was practising his jumps. He couldn't see us watching through the thick bush on the other side of the wire fence.

'I can do this myself,' I said. 'I'm the fastest and once I get him down near the creek, he won't be able to pass me. How you going to bring him down?'

'Got it sussed,' Roddy said. 'We'll make him stack and once he's down, we got a rope to hog-tie him. Then we'll totally teach him not to fuck with us. 'You sure you don't want Cudgy with you?'

'I'm good ... just be ready.'

'Give us ten minutes,' Soupy said. 'Lead him down the track this side of the creek. The left fork.'

'Choice. This oughta be fun,' I said and they took off down towards the creek and I headed around to the quarry gate.

Once I entered, I cut the motor on my bike and slipped my helmet off so I could hear his bike over at the jumps on the other side of the rim. I had an idea, if only I could sneak up on him. I picked up a nice piece of blue rock, half the size of my palm and rode slowly down one of the old quarry ramps below a small dirt embankment, where I hid behind a clump of bushes.

He rode over. I thought he'd seen me but instead he zipped past without turning his head. I watched him slide his back wheel out up the top of the track and head back towards me. I had to be patient. When he was within a hundred metres or so, I kick-started the bike, dropped the clutch and went kamikaze, full pelt straight at him. We must have looked like jousting knights as I piffed the rock at his face. He turned his head and the shale bounced off his new helmet and I took off around the rim of the quarry as fast as my little motorbike could take me without looking behind. I'd left the gate open just a whisker, enough to get my bike through and then I pulled it shut behind me before tearing off through the bush, down toward the gully where the others were waiting.

The long winding track made it difficult for him to catch up. I was flying through the trees, knowing he'd have to ride pretty tight and hard to catch me. I made it down to the fork in the track, skidded left, and took off again flat-out parallel to the creek, fanging it up through the gears until I reached full speed. I couldn't see the other guys, surely they hadn't ditched me – I didn't fully trust Roddy.

I could hear Debono's engine screaming up behind, then a rope passed beneath me. I thought that was strange, then I heard his bike rev fully and I knew somehow he'd fallen off. I locked the back wheel up and stopped and turned my head. Debono's riderless bike came straight toward me then veered left and hit a tree. Debono was on the ground.

'Get him,' Soupy yelled and all three sprung from the trees and began kicking him in the legs and back. Soupy wore his leather boots. Roddy wore a similar pair like cowboy boots and they were sticking those boots in hard by the time I got off my bike and ran up to join in. Debono lay on his side. I thought he was cowering up in a ball so I kicked the side of his head and heard a gut-wrenching click, a crack I can still hear to this day. We all heard it but kept going, I don't know why. We kicked him all over, just like he did to Roddy and Soupy. But he didn't fight back.

Then Roddy surprised us all when he started yelling, 'Hey, hey, stop! Stop guys, stop!' He had his arms spread out, pushing us back. I had no idea why he wanted to stop.

'Guys. Guys. Step back!'

Soupy kicked him one more time in the arse, Roddy shoved him backwards. 'He's not moving.'

'Get up ya weak dog,' I said and stepped over Debono so I could see his face. His helmet had no visor. The eyes were open and moist, his face was covered in dust and blood trickled from the bottom corner of his mouth. Yellow and purple bruising had coloured his neck around the chin strap and seemed to darken further, right before my eyes.

'Why isn't he moving?' Cudgy said.

'What the hell did you guys do?' I asked.

'Us? His neck totally clicked when you kicked him, Gillo,' Soupy said. 'I heard it. We all did.'

'Me? Everyone kicked him. The bruise … why is his neck bruised like that?'

None of them said anything at first. I recalled running over the rope.

'We … we stopped him … that's all,' Roddy said.

I glared at him in disbelief. 'With the rope?'

'How else were we—?'

'You got him in the neck. You totally fuckin' necked him, you idiots.'

'It was you, Roddy,' Soupy said. 'You held the rope too high.'

'Don't blame me, it was your idea, arsehole.'

Soupy pushed him. 'Bullshit tossbag ... you're the one who brought the rope.'

'You held it too so don't fucking push me you skinny little faggot—' Then the situation appeared to grip him and he ignored Soupy and knelt down. 'DEBONO! DEBONO! WAKE UP!'

'Don't touch his neck,' Cudgy said. 'He might ... we might have to get him to a hospital or something—'

I shook my head. 'He's ... he's—' I tried to say dead. It wouldn't come out. I think I was frozen with fear.

'Shit shit ... shit! Fuck! Is he ... dead?' Soupy said, his lips were shuddering. He circled the body. 'Oh fuck ...' He held his head in his hands. 'What the hell we gonna do?'

'DEBONO!' Roddy knelt down and touched the skin on his face, lifting his head gently before he slipped his hand away. The head flopped back to the ground under the weight of the helmet, the eyes watery and glassed over, wide open.

'He's not moving,' Roddy said. 'Car'n Debono! DEBONO!'

'He's dead ... he's dead. Shit ... Christ ... what've we done?' Cudgy said, whimpering with his face cupped in his hands.

'Can't be. Give him a tick,' Roddy said. 'He might just be stunned or something. I dunno.' He unclipped Debono's helmet, more blood seeped from his mouth to the dirt.

I saw the doubt and horror in Roddy's face as he stepped back from the grisly sight. Reality struck. All four of us stood there watching Debono for several minutes, could've been ten for all the good it would do. I'd never seen a dead body before.

"Can't say that tomorrow, son." Came Old Nick's crisp, radio-like voice in my head.

I wanted Debono to move, I really did, and even said a quiet prayer to myself. I knew he'd come around eventually and this would soon be all right. But he never did. Nothing changed, except the cold wind floating down the gully, awakening my skin. Trees gave a deathly rustle. Milky, vacant eyes gazed up at the forest like those kangaroo eyes at the back of Nick's hut. I stared at what I now knew was a body. The eyes forever locked on the distant.

I tasted sick, it rose up in my mouth, dizziness came, my brow burned. I reached out and found a tree to steady myself as the rolling motion started. I buckled over. Vomit exploded. Someone else started barfing too, I heard the chundering and the splashing, which only served to make me chuck again. I coughed and gagged; my body felt the need to lurch my intestines out through my throat.

'Oh shit, Gillings, you grot,' Roddy said. 'Man. You fuckin' chucked on him.'

I didn't answer because my vision was blurred. After I'd spat the remainder of the puke from my mouth, I was able to see again. Spew had splashed on his face and helmet. Cudgy was bent over spitting onto the ground, having chucked up too. I had to do something about those eyes so I unbuttoned my flannelette shirt and placed it over Debono's head. I didn't want to see those eyes any longer.

Wind gusted, chilling the sweat inside my tee shirt against my skin. Some sort of death rattle went through me right to the bones. I crunched my teeth together and had to wait for it to pass before I said, 'He's dead ... we've fucked up. We gotta tell the cops.' I became cold in an instant. Goosebumps rose on every pore of my bare arms, sending me into shivering spasms but I couldn't take my shirt back. Those eyes beneath it were colder. They told of what we had done.

Roddy rubbed his chin and studied us all. 'If he's dead ... know what that means if we tell the cops? Means we go to juvy.'

'What are you on about?' My words came out slow. I spat a little more saliva and puke. 'It's an accident.' I glanced at

Cudgy. His lips had turned blue, his face as pale as a ghost gum.

'No it wasn't,' Roddy said. 'We killed him. We didn't mean to but—'

I held my head in my hands. 'We can't just leave him here.' I couldn't believe what he was saying. 'We gotta tell the cops, man.'

'What? That you led him down here and we put a rope across the track and hung him. Good one, Gillings. Think juvy dipshit.'

'Juvy?'

Roddy leant in close to my face and this time he spoke loud and slow. 'JU VE NILE DETEN SHONE FUCKHEAD. KNOW WHAT THAT MEANS? MEANS PRISON IF WE'RE CAUGHT … YOU COMPRE-FUCKIN'-HENDAY GILLINGS? GET A GRIP FOR GOD'S SAKE.'

I held his gaze. Prison. I couldn't go to prison.

Roddy kept going. 'Means we're all going to Turana Detention Centre … till we're old enough, then they'll send us to Pentridge. By the time you get out Gillings, you'll be shittin' donuts. You wanna go through all that? You wanna get your arse pumped?'

Surely they don't really do that in prison, I remember thinking.

'We didn't mean it … we … we … didn't mean it,' Cudgy said, his voice fading. Saliva was strung between his lips and I thought he was going to burst into tears.

'Don't matter. We did it,' Soupy said. He too was whispering. 'We're history big time if we tell anyone.'

Why was he whispering? I began to peer around through the trees for shadows … shadows in the late afternoon shadows that already seemed to be moving. Would *they* come out from those shadows? Cops, followed by the rest of the world. What lay ahead for us?

'We … we can just say he ran away,' Roddy said in a low voice. 'We gotta say he told us he planned on running away … or something. Let's figure this out.'

We stood around in silence, me replaying each word that had been said.

'Back to the clubhouse,' Roddy said.

'What … Roddy? What if someone comes along?' Even though we hardly ever saw anyone down here, I felt sure the minute we left, someone would surely come along the track simply because there was a dead body there.

'I said back to the clubhouse,' Roddy ordered. 'We gotta meet … think this through and I can't concentrate while I'm looking at him like that. The clubhouse is the place to meet.'

He was right about one thing. Rule 6 stated all meetings must be held in the clubhouse and the blowies had started attacking us, and the puke. I wanted to get out of there, but didn't want to leave Debono. Also, Meatlips had said he'd be coming along soon. He'd know what to do. But what about the body?

'We can't just ditch him here,' Soupy said, stealing words off my tongue.

Then Roddy picked up the feet and just like that, he began pulling Debono off the track.

'Don't move him … you can't move him,' Cudgy said, flapping his arms about, then he flung them up and I heard them slap on his thighs in defeat and frustration.

'He's dead, ya moron,' Roddy said.

Cudgy was right. The moment after he touched the body, the whole scenario changed like the wind. This became even more serious, if that was possible. We all stood by as Roddy dragged Debono by the legs as far as he could down to the edge of the creek, which was nothing more than mud and a trickle of water running through reeds. He began snapping low branches and fronds off ferns, using them to cover Debono.

'You moved the body,' Cudgy said aloud. His voice echoed in the dead of the forest.

'Shut up. Someone'll hear you,' I said, despite knowing full well no one else was around except for us.

Cudgy pulled at the skin on his face. 'We're fucked. We can't get out of this. If they find out you moved him, they'll wanna know why … and they *will* find out.' With his foot he frantically began to smooth the dirt over where the body had been. Then he broke off a branch and swept it over the tracks Roddy had made by dragging the body.

'Car'n … let's get to the clubhouse and sort this out,' Cudgy said. 'You're right, Gillo. We gotta tell someone, just have to figure out who. Give me a hand with his bike.'

'Okay.' I felt a little better. Cudgy wanted to do the right thing. Meatlips might even be up at the clubhouse by now, waiting. He'd know what to do. Together, we lifted Debono's bike and walked it into the bush. We laid more branches over it, then I stared at the scene. If anyone came down here they'd know. It was obvious to me something had been hidden.

'Let's get outa here,' Roddy said. We kick-started our bikes and began to ride off slowly in single file, but I only heard Cudgy's bike behind me. I stopped and looked back. Roddy had caught Soupy by the arm, their bikes idling as they spoke. They saw me and started riding again. We continued up toward the quarry, but I knew those two were scheming. Roddy, my one time best mate who I no longer trusted, and Soupy. I'd always known Soupy was going to get into major trouble one day and here I was, in the deepest shit imaginable with him. As I approached the quarry gates, I knew the only way to end this now was to just keep riding flat-out until I reached the cop shop. None of them would catch me. But I didn't and I changed my life. Instead, I relied on Meatlips being in the clubhouse and went back through the slight opening in those gates. No one else but me was to blame. I chose to let our fates hinge on each other.

CHAPTER 11

There was no sign of Meatlips when we climbed the ladder. My throat was as dry as a nun. Bruce Botwin taught me that saying. He worked for Dad when we needed an extra hand and always said *"he was as dry as a nun"* around knock off time. I assumed it was because nuns weren't supposed to drink alcohol, although I must confess, I never asked him what he meant. He scared me a bit and I didn't say much around him.

I glanced over my shoulder at the far corner of the quarry. We could only see a very small patch of green surface, but with the sun gleaming off it, right then I was so thirsty, that water looked good enough to drink.

Inside the clubhouse no one said a word until Roddy, the V.P. picked up the mash hammer.

'I declare this meeting open.' He hit the floorboards.

'What meeting?' I said. 'Only Meatlips can open a meeting. Let's wait.' I wanted Meatlips around. He'd make them see the right decision was to tell the cops. I thought of Mr. and Mrs. Debono. Would they believe their boy ran away? My mind was *actually* thinking it might be the best thing to say. They were Italian; I'd seen both Godfather movies. His dad might know Italian criminals.

'As V.P. I have decided we need to have this meeting, now.' Before I could say anything, Roddy pointed to the charter on the wall. 'Rule 7, Gillings.'

Rule 7: In the unlikely event the president is absent, meetings will be chaired by the vice president.

'He's on his way.'

'He's not here, Gillings. Tough shit. Meeting's open.'

'I second it,' Cudgy said.

'Me too,' Soupy replied.

I sat still.

Soupy looked towards Roddy. 'What are we gonna do about this?'

'Who agrees it wasn't an accident?' Roddy's hand was already in the air. Soupy followed, so did Cudgy. I relented and put up my hand.

'Who agrees we can't tell anyone?'

All the other hands stayed up, except mine.

'Rule 5, Gillings,' Roddy said. 'You're out-voted.'

Rule 5: All motions (notwithstanding Rules 3 &10) must be carried by a majority vote.

I glared at Cudgy. 'You total chicken shit. You said we're gonna decide who to tell.'

'The club has ruled different,' Roddy said.

'What? You can't do that without Meatlips. Someone's dead, for Christ's sake.'

Soupy turned his nose up at me. 'Get in the corner Gillo ... you reek of spew.'

I had spew on the cuffs of my jeans and on my runners. 'Get fucked. We're in this together, if I have to smell it, so do you.'

Roddy continued on. 'We can't tell anyone, especially Meatlips. No one will believe it was an accident. One slip up and we're screwed. They'll put us in separate rooms and belt us over the heads with phone books until they find out what they think the truth is. Did it to my older cousin. Slammed him with a phone book till he dobbed his mates in, and all they did was brick a shop window. Cops aren't dumb you know. They take you to Melbourne, phone books are thicker there. Then it's off to juvy. Turana ... where they put the maddest kids in the state. Kids who murder and kill definitely go there until they're old enough to go to Pentridge Prison.'

Pentridge. The word sent shivers down my spine. *"Phone books over the head,"* came Nick's voice again. He'd lived two states away and said the same thing. It must be true. Surely the cops wouldn't do that to kids.

'All we have to do is start a rumour,' Roddy said. 'We just say he's been braggin' about running away.'

'Yeah,' the other two said. Captain Spineless, Cudgy was doing his follow the leader bullshit as usual, even when a boy was lying dead in the forest and we were responsible. Meatlips would be here soon, I told myself.

'This is what we say when they ask,' Roddy said. 'He's told us all at different times he's been thinking about running away. We also have to say he wasn't here at the quarry. Haven't seen him all day. Got that Gillings?'

It was true. We were the only kids that hung out at the quarry, so no one else would've seen him except us. 'What about his bike?'

'We'll work that out later?' Roddy said. 'Be piss easy to get rid of.'

I shook my head. 'This is like … murder.'

'He ran away, Gillings. Get it through ya thick head. If we're caught, all of us go to juvy. He's dead. We can't fix that for him but we can fix it for ourselves so we don't get locked up. That's what we gotta concentrate on. I bet a zillion kids have done this and you know why we haven't heard of it happening before?' Roddy shot his gaze directly at me. 'Cause they get away with it.'

A motorbike approached. Debono's bike was the first one to come to my mind before the seriousness of this situation swamped me once again. I recognised the sound of Meatlips's XR. Cudgy stood up and looked out the same window his prick relations used to shoot wild pigs out of. 'It's Meatlips. What do we tell him?'

'Nothing,' Roddy said.

'Why not,' I shot back. 'He's one of us. He's our president.'

'Because he wasn't there. He's the only one with nuthin' to lose. Who agrees?' Roddy and Soupy shot their hands up again. Cudgy's stayed down, like mine. The bike stopped. The engine cut. They glared at us. Suddenly I had Cudgy on my side, he too was relying on Meatlips to straighten the others out.

As I studied Roddy and Soupy, I recalled them talking back on the track. They'd already worked everything out between themselves. I cursed myself for not riding past the gates, I'd be at the cops by now spilling my guts out.

Roddy's face tightened right up. 'Who votes we don't tell Meatlips.' He thrust his clenched fist up. Soupy followed. 'Make up your minds, you two.' I kept my hand down, knowing Cudgy would do whatever Meatlips said; that was a given.

'Hurry up,' Soupy said, but it was too late. We could hear him climbing the steps.

'Don't you say nothing,' Roddy said with desperation welded into his face. His jaw tensed even more but it was two on two. Meatlips must be told and then surely we'd have to do the right thing. Tell the cops. Tell his oldies. Tell everyone it was just a stupid, horrible accident.

Meatlips poked his head up from the ladder and looked around before climbing through the floor opening. I knew he sensed something was going on. Bewdy, I thought. He'll straighten this out, properly.

Meatlips focused on Roddy with the gavel in his hand. He cast wary eyes around at us. No one said a word. Not even hello. A dead give-away.

'What's going on fellas?'

'Nothing,' Soupy said. He pulled his cigarettes from his pocket. 'Just having a smoke.'

Meatlips sniffed. 'Smells rank in here.'

'Meet Chuck Chunder,' Soupy said and nodded at me.

Meatlips looked at Roddy's fingers wrapped around the hammer. He climbed up all the way and stood in the middle, gazing down on us because we were all seated on the floor. He had a can of solo. I almost died with relief.

'Give me a sip?' He passed the can.

'Keep it,' he said and reached down and slowly slid the mash hammer from Roddy's fingers.

'Someone tell me what's going on here?'

No one spoke.

Meatlips glared straight at Cudgy. 'Cudgy?'

'Debono's dead.'

'You weak cunt,' Roddy spat. 'We agreed—'

'No we didn't.' As if to enforce his point, Cudgy buttoned his lips and shook his head fiercely.

I felt a great relief as a sly smile shifted on Meatlips's purple cheek. The birthmark reminded me of the horrible bruising around Debono's neck. I felt sure Meatlips would tell the others what I had already told them.

'Oh … hoh … tell me yous guys are kidding.'

We all stared at him, shaking our heads.

'Shit, yous guys … c'mon?'

'Fully,' Cudgy said.

'Totally,' I said.

'Oh fuck! You're … you're serious. How? When?'

''Bout half hour ago,' I said. Roddy and Soupy burned holes through me with their eyes. 'We did it.'

'What the … what are yous on about?'

'Roddy moved the body,' I said.

'Roddy. Tell me you didn't do something as stupid as that. Tell me this isn't real. For fuck's sake tell me the joke here, guys.'

'It was an accident,' Cudgy said.

'Holy fuck!' Meatlips ran his fingers through his hair.

Soupy shifted on his arse bones, resting his weight on one arm and staring at the floor. 'It's true.'

I looked at Roddy. He was all alone. Meatlips was the most mature amongst us. I felt sure we'd be able to sort through this and work out who to tell and what to tell. I told him everything from start to finish.

Meatlips absorbed it all. 'So that's what this meeting's about. That's why you got the gavel, huh Roddy? Tell me what you decided to do?'

Roddy turned to Soupy. 'We can't tell no one. We gotta say he ran away, right Soupy?'

'Right on,' Soupy said. 'We'll spread some rumours. Go down the pinnies, start saying he's knicked off, run away … you know. Just have to say other kids told us, so it don't seem like we started the rumours. Stacks of other kids have ran away … should be a cinch.' Then his eyes fell on me. 'If we all stick together, that is.'

I studied Meatlips as he rubbed his chin.

Huh! I thought, questioning why wasn't he saying something. Surely he couldn't be thinking about going along with this.

'My older brother did it … ran away twice, years ago,' Cudgy said. 'No-one had any idea where the hell he was until he come home. Still don't. We just need to get our story straight, that's all. Someone else can say they saw him with a girl from outa town … a punk girl … older or sumptin' … that's it, older. Say she had safety pins through her nose and all that shit. We could say he's been getting a root. We could say we saw em' rooting down here … at the quarry.'

'Can't say he was at the quarry,' Meatlips said.

What? I was unable to believe he could possibly even think of siding with them, but to my horror, Meatlips nodded.

'It's off to juvy if you guys are caught. We're not going to take a vote. Yous guys are right. We can't tell anyone yet till we decide what to do. Where is he … the body?'

'At the creek,' I said, 'but … Meatlips, come on, you can't agree to this—'

'You're fucked otherwise, Gillo. Life's over. Let's go down there and take a look. Leave the bikes here. We'll walk down in case anyone's around.'

I wanted to run, to jump on my bike and get out of there but instead I followed because deep down, I didn't want my life to change. As we walked through the bush in silence I wished with all my heart Debono had woken up and gone home, but when we reached the body, his hands were white. Solid concrete white. Meatlips lifted the shirt. A swarm of blowflies scattered off his face in the fading light and Meatlips flicked the rest off with the shirt. The neck was blue and purple and yellow. A strange, uneasy, almost thrilling sense swept through me. Perhaps because I'd seen the body earlier, perhaps because we had a way forward I couldn't see before. We now had a story and believed we could get away with it. I was becoming more accustomed to our predicament.

'Shit,' Meatlips said. He had this eerie smile. 'Neck must be broken. They'll think yous hung him.'

We did, I thought to myself, then tried to retain the thought as something positive because I also heard that crack of his neck when I kicked him. It echoed through my mind.

Meatlips handled the scene of a dead body, no problems. For me, it seemed easier the second time.

'You seen a dead body before?' I asked.

'Yeah … my granddad … they popped the lid at the funeral.'

'Serious? What … what do we do?'

'Bury him. Do what the others said. Say he ran away.'

I think by that time I realised we'd taken too long already and the cops would know that, somehow. I was beginning to accept the others were right. I knew it was crazy and totally wrong to go along with this, but another part of me had known what he was going to say.

'This is what a strong club would do,' Meatlips said. 'Stick together. Yous guys are in big shit if we don't, and you've already moved the body. Once you move the body, they'll know you got something to hide. Cops 'll know it's been moved. We get rid of everything. No one will ever know he hasn't run away.'

'What'd I say,' Roddy said.

'Bury him … yeah,' Soupy said.

'They won't start looking for him till tomorrow.' Meatlips stood over the body holding his chin. 'Yous reckon this happened nearly an hour ago. Cops can tell, you know … the exact time of death. You go and tell 'em now, they'll know he's been sitting here for a while and yous have been planning a story. It's way too late. We do this tonight. Meet at the quarry gates. Eleven thirty with shovels. Should give us stacks of time.'

'Yeah … we have to,' Cudgy said.

'Guys—?' I said.

'Listen Gillo,' Meatlips said. 'Roddy's right. They may believe it's an accident, what if they don't … and you can still do some juvy time for an accident. It's a bad place. Kids ten times worse than him.' He nodded at the body.

I tried to imagine kids ten times worse than Debono. I pictured him scowling down at me from the aisle in the bus. He really was a mean kid.

Kids ten times worse.

Then I saw his father's face, his mother's face. He had an older sister, Angela, seventeen, and here's me, wondering how to cover up killing her only brother. There was so much depth to this. It would be better for them to think he ran away. If we did this right, no one would ever know.

'They're your mates,' Meatlips said to me. 'You going to lag 'em all in or stick with your mates? Once you tell anyone, you can't go back. No more club, no more riding, no more races … no more mates … no more …' He threw his hands up. 'You can rule out girls and all that shit. I'm telling ya, it's juvy for the lot of yous.'

I began to believe he was right. 'What about his motorbike?' I asked.

'Dump it in the quarry,' Cudgy said. 'It's deep. No one's ever gonna find it.'

'Cops might once they come sniffing about,' Meatlips said.

'I'll take it to my joint,' Roddy said. 'Only take a few hours to strip it down.'

Meatlips nodded. 'Do it straight away. And no selling any parts. Cops 'll trace 'em. Bury anything with a serial number in a hole down the back of your joint.'

Roddy's mum's property was ten acres. The back half was fenced off where they ran a few sheep, behind that was a strip of bushland alongside the railway line. There were plenty of places for him to bury the bike.

'I'll come get it after dark tonight.'

'Just be careful no one sees you riding it,' Meatlips said.

Since Roddy's dad died of cancer, he could do what he wanted. His mum drank all day every day and Roddy spent most of his time in his dad's shed. His mum didn't have a clue what he was up to out there and wouldn't know whose bike was whose. And also, his dad had left him just about every tool known to man. It was all starting to fit together and make a strange kind of sense. I was actually beginning to think this might work.

'We can send a note to his family saying he ran away.' Roddy said.

'No way,' Meatlips said. 'They'll suss it out and know if the note didn't come from Debono.'

'How?' Roddy asked.

'Simple. Won't have his fingerprints on it. It'll have yours instead, fucking dumbass.'

'I mean wipe it down first,' Roddy said, angrily.

'Yeah well, saw a murderer do it on a cop show,' Meatlips said. 'Columbo I reckon. He figured it out and caught the murderer, even though the fingerprints weren't on a record. Got them off a drinking glass from the killer's home.'

'We could use gloves, or type it,' Soupy said.

'Still won't have his fingerprints on it,' Meatlips said, 'and the cops can tell which typewriter it came from. What if there's no typewriter or nothing in his house? And who would typewrite a run away note anyway? No notes. I mean it. Just rumours, that's all. We meet tonight at the quarry gates. Bring torches and shovels. Are we all together on this?"

I stared down at the body, knowing what was right, but also knowing what was easier.

'Gillo,' Meatlips said. 'You in?

'Gillo?'

'Don't be piss weak, Gillo,' Soupy said. 'He's dead. We gotta fix things up for ourselves.'

'Gillings ... you in?' Roddy asked.

What if I'm not? I suddenly thought.

But then I knew if we told someone, everything we had come to know would change. They might not believe us, and then what? Juvy? Pentridge?

'Gillo,' Meatlips said, 'you part of this club or not?'

I eyeballed them all then dropped my head, muttering the words, 'I'm in.'

CHAPTER 12

'Where's Mum?' I asked Dad when I walked up the drive, nervous as all hell. Trying to act as normal as I possibly could under extreme circumstances. The tailgate was down on the back of the ute. He'd just swept it clean and was about to begin re-loading all his work gear in front of the garage.

Dad leaned on the broom and said, 'Inside ironing freaking tea towels, whatever they do in-doors.'

He grinned and pulled on his beer. I made a feeble attempt to laugh. All that came out was a guilt-ridden, sort of dud chortle. The taste of sick rolled in my mouth.

"Dad. Something terrible has happened," I desperately wanted to tell him.

He jumped up into the back of the ute. 'Pass me Vitas Shovelaitis?'

To lighten the mood at work, Dad nicknamed the shovels after the pro tennis player, Vitas Gerulaitis. I passed him up the two that were on the ground, the ones we used for work. I glanced sideways. More shovels stood in the front corner of the shed.

'Pickus Dickus. Crowbarius Maximus.'

I passed him up the pick and the crowbar. Ever since he'd taken me to see Monty Python's The Life of Brian at the picture theatre in Bushmore, some tools had been granted Roman names. Because of the anti-Christian theme of the film, he lied to Mum and told her we were going to see Jaws 2, instead. *"Guess it's okay to see people chomped up by a shark, but don't knock God,"* he'd said at the time.

I was in no mood for his jokes.

'You all right?'

'Huh! What do you mean? Fine. Just tired.'

'Well, go inside then, see your mother.'

My heart skipped. Shit. Had something happened, already? 'Why?'

'It's dinnertime. School's tomorrow.'

'Oh.'

'Knockrometer.'

I passed him up the sledgehammer.

'Give me a lift with that toolbox.' He jumped down and we both hauled the main toolbox up into the ute. I stood back away from him as much as I could, worried he'd smell the puke but he didn't mention it. I told him I needed to go to the toilet so I hurried inside, glad to be out of his way. Had he sensed something was wrong in only a few seconds? Perhaps Debono's oldies had already been around asking about Tony, but then Dad would surely have said something. I tried to convince myself they knew nothing. Why would his family come here, anyway? Tony hadn't been to our house in ages and Meatlips said they wouldn't be around looking until tomorrow, at the earliest.

I kicked my runners off at the door and walked inside to the smell of Sunday roast.

'Hi Jackie dear,' Mum said. 'Where've you been, it's almost dark?'

I couldn't say I was at the quarry. 'Down the street … the pinnies.' Was the first of many lies to come. 'Just busting—' I hurried to the toilet before any more questions were fired at me.

Once I made it to the safety of my room I changed out of my stinking jeans into some trackies. I grabbed a wiper from the laundry and cleaned my shoes, but had to get my jeans out. They'd stink up my room in no time, so I found a plastic bag in my cupboard and stashed them out past the laundry door. Then I went back inside, laid down on my bed and shut my eyes.

Debono's dead face appeared.

Juvy, juvy, juvy. The word would not leave my mind. The others were right. This was the only way out, the only way to lead a normal life.

At dinner my peas went down like balls of cardboard. Chicken tasted gross. So did Mum's gravy. Previously, it had always been the best gravy I'd ever had; better than they made at the pub because she often bragged that she used Vegemite for a base and a lamb hock instead of stock cubes. I excused myself after a few mouthfuls and went straight into the bathroom and closed the door, so they wouldn't hear me doing something as weird as brushing my teeth halfway through dinner.

I came back out and struggled through half a potato.

'Jack, you okay?' Mum asked. 'You're a bit pale.'

'Not feeling too well.'

'At least eat your vegetables, honey.'

'I can't.' I couldn't face her, couldn't look sideways at Dad. I said nothing to Tommy and focused on my food, despite being barely able to stomach it.

'Don't you think you're going to pull this off, young man.'

I shot an instant glance at her. This time my heart leapt almost out of my throat. How did she know? Who had told already? Cudgy. It had to be Cudgy.

'You better not be foxing. School's tomorrow and you're going. I didn't come down in the last shower you know.'

Thank God, I thought. Tommy and I had to have temperatures off the scale to get a day off school and she thought I was trying to chuck a sickie to get a long weekend.

'I'll be right.' I kept looking down at my plate. Truth was, I had no idea how I'd be feeling in the morning. We had a long night ahead of us and I'd never gone without sleeping. I also had no intention of missing school. For one thing, I had to help start the rumours Debono had run away and secondly, if I missed a day and something went wrong tonight and Debono was found to be dead, they might check the roster and see who's not at school for the day. I learnt that from an episode earlier in the year when a couple of kids decided to pull a bomb scare. They rang the school and said there was a bomb in the cleaner's room. We all got sent home, but the staff went through the roster and saw who was away on that day. Those kids got busted because they were known to hang around together, and their parents had no idea they were wagging.

Dad slurped his gravy, like soup. Mum wrapped a hunk of chicken in bread and sopped it in her own gravy, and ate it. Tommy gnawed on a thighbone and stuffed a potato down with the other hand.

I could have told them. All I had to do was open my mouth and begin. It was best I do it in front of Tommy, too. He would find out sometime, eventually. I wondered how the others were doing. I stared at the phone, waiting for it to ring. Silence. Cudgy would have told his stepmum by now and the police would surely come around soon. All I had to do was speak. Easy. Open my mouth. The truth, my way out of this was one sentence away. I only had to say the words, "*it was an accident.*"

Juvy.

I opened my mouth, stabbed a pea onto my fork and swallowed it whole.

CHAPTER 13

After dinner, my focus once again was on trying to act normal, like nothing was out of place. Tommy and I had a game of draughts on the lounge room floor and when he went to bed at seven thirty, I also shuffled down the passage to my room.

'Have an early night, honey,' Mum said.

I waited fifteen minutes for Mum and Dad to settle into their Sunday night TV before sneaking out through the laundry to the garage. It was better to get a shovel ready now, than have Dad think there was a burglar in the middle of the night. I figured if he followed me outside, I could say I was checking the chook pen. Foxes had been spotted down Whispering Creek lately. Rex followed me and I let him come, rather than have my oldies hear me telling the dog to stay. Dad had pulled down the garage roller door, so I went around to the side door and crept in through the dark, trying to remember where everything was so I wouldn't make a racket by bumping into Dad's welding gear. Oxy bottles and hoses and stuff were lying about, there were also stormy pipes on the floor. I hadn't even thought to bring the torch I kept under my bed. My eyes adjusted easily. I found a shovel and turfed it over the back fence. Then I wheeled my old pushy down the back too, so I could make my escape later on down the creek. Rex and I slipped back inside, unnoticed. This was going to be a long night. I couldn't wait until it was over. I didn't know then, that this would never be over.

I tried reading but words wouldn't stick in my brain. Nine o'clock followed eight. Each hour seemed like it took two to pass. Every nerve ending tingled. I saw Debono's stone cold face, those blank eyes. Someone walked up the hall to the toilet, I could tell it was Mum. I shut my book, closed my eyes and rolled over. Another opportunity to call her in and tell her everything, passed by. Instead, I pulled the doona up tight, to make it look like I was asleep. Finally just after ten I heard footsteps as my parents went to bed. Pretty soon eleven o'clock came around. My escape was well planned. I told Rex to stay. He slept on my bed most nights (some nights he slept with Tommy) and if I threw my doona over him, he normally wouldn't move because he liked being under the doona. I closed my bedroom door almost fully, so if he needed to get out to the toilet he could do so by nudging the door open. I'd snuck out before without him and hooked up with the guys for roof-rocking expeditions in the middle of the night, and always came home to find him still on my bed. We hadn't done it for maybe a year or so, instead, we had grown out of roof-rocking and moved onto burying a dead kid.

Whispering Creek hummed of a cold, howling wind, like voices. I waited behind a tree, listening for the voices, peering through the darkness toward the fence line at the rear of Debono's property. Waiting for his father to reveal himself. I don't know how long I waited, terrified, knowing Debono's old man was out there somewhere looking for his son. A ghostly figure leapt our wire fence. I shit myself until I realised it was Rex. It was useless to take him back, I'd get busted for sure. He knew something was going on. I hoped no one else in my family had the same intuition as my dog. Rex twisted his head and gave a questioning whine. 'Come on,' I said, feeling a little more secure. My mother's voice tapped away in my mind. *"Take Rex with you when you go into the forest."*

What about when I'm going to bury a dead kid from our street? A kid from my school. A kid we all knew. Was I destined to feel like this for the rest of my life?

Across the other side of the creek was a narrow tract of bushland, beyond that was farming land and forest. Silver clouds drifted beneath an almost full moon. The night sky was bright as I rode with the shovel slung over my shoulder beneath the snow-white cockatoos sleeping high in the gum trees. I studied the tones of pitch-blackness between the trees, watching, expecting movement, expecting searchers. Dad was a volunteer in the local fire brigade. I assumed they would be called upon to take up a search and of course, nothing had happened yet. I felt safe beneath those silver clouds – silver linings for how long – providing enough light for me to switch the headlight off on my pushy. It was best to ride in the dark.

I avoided the streets and took the long way through the bush tracks, skirting the town. I only had to cross one road, the Coast Road. When I reached it, I got off my bike and hid behind a tree to check both ways. No one.

I met the others at the quarry. All except for Meatlips.

'What'd you bring that mutt for?' Roddy said.

'He's just a dog. Can't exactly tell anyone.'

'No one else better have followed you, Gillings.'

'Course not. Where the hell's Meatlips?'

'Reckons it's best he didn't come,' Roddy said. I noticed he was holding a handsaw. 'Anyway, we know what we gotta do.'

'What's with the saw? Fuck! Don't tell me—'

'Tree roots, dickhead. We're gonna strike tree roots when we dig.'

I should have thought of tree roots, my dad being a plumber.

'Heard any news yet?' Cudgy said. 'Anything going on in your street?'

'Nah. Nothing. No one's come round. Phone ain't rung. What about you guys?'

'Town's dead. Saw no one on the way over here,' Soupy said. 'Let's do this. I start my paper round in a few hours.' He led us into the blackened forest. We all had torches and split up to make sure no one else was around. Rex wasn't barking, though. A good sign we were alone.

I had visions of the body not being there again, and I admit to feeling a weird form of comfort when we found Debono exactly where we left him. Cudgy stuck his spade in the ground near the body. 'Here,' he said and outlined a grave on a level section of the gully. 'Let's dig, two each end.'

The ground was soft. Having a plumber for a dad, I was certainly the best digger and the hole grew and grew. Petrified, I kept shining my torch into the night that filled the gaps between those surrounding trees. That hollow darkness represented our futures in some way. If anyone walked out, we didn't have a future. Trees swayed in the gully breeze, boughs creaked and no animals came by. Only the moon stared as we took shifts. Soon we were down to our knees.

'How far do we go?' I asked.

'Meatlips reckons six foot,' Roddy said.

'Fuckin' kiddin' me.'

'Gotta, Gillings. Anyone bring a tape?

'Nope.'

'Gotta be six feet,' Cudgy said.

'Why?' Soupy asked. 'We only got four hours left.'

'It's what they do. Grave diggers. Don't you know nothin'?' Roddy said.

'Shut the fuck up,' Soupy said. 'Six feet's a crock of shit. We're never gonna make it.'

'Have to,' Roddy shot back. 'Animals 'll dig him up otherwise. I'm five-seven. Gotta go a deeper than me.'

'You're not five-seven,' I said.

'Am so.'

'Five ton, maybe,' Soupy said and we all laughed, except Roddy. He cracked it big time.

We dug by torchlight, cutting the tree roots as we went. No one thought to bring water and I was forced to grin and bear my thirst, again. Aerogard would have been useful too.

Mozzies soon found us, being near the creek. They drove us nuts all night. Suddenly we hit harder ground, clay. I should have brought a crow bar. All we could do was thrust the shovels in and chip away, they almost bounced back up at us with each strike, partly because we were becoming tired. Roddy and I were in the trench. It was three thirty in the morning and we could only work for another hour and a half, tops, before we'd have to leave enough time to fill the grave in and try to hide it.

Cudgy had already dug some clumps of grass up during his break from grave digging. His plan was to plant them in the top of the grave, which was now up to my stomach. 'We're not gonna get this done,' I said, wiping sweat off my brow.

'Keep going,' our V.P. said. 'We're committed.'

So we dug full on for the next hour, chipping away until we couldn't get much deeper.

'Let's just chuck him in and backfill it,' Soupy said.

Cudgy rested on his shovel, panting. 'Reckon it's only about four and a half feet.'

'Not coming back tomorrow,' Soupy said. 'Has to be enough.'

'Give us a hand.' Roddy was holding one of Debono's feet.

I grabbed the other leg. Cudgy grabbed an arm and a crack filled the night. Roddy frowned. 'Careful, for Christ sake. Stop being a dick, Cudgy. You'll break him.'

'Like that'll make a diff,' Cudgy said and yanked harder. The arm broke again; still he continued to pull the body around. We dragged the legs and tipped him into the trench. The arm stuck up. 'Someone get down there, straighten him up and stick that arm down properly,' Cudgy said.

'You,' I said. 'I ain't getting in there.'

To my surprise Roddy thrust a shovel down on the arm, then jumped in on top of the body and wriggled it around until it lay flat, then hoisted himself out. 'Start filling it in. We gotta split.'

104

'Shouldn't we say something?' Cudgy said.

'We should,' Soupy replied. 'Gather round.'

We all stood at the edge of the gravesite, heads bowed.

'Have fun pushing up daisies, ya prick,' Soupy said and shovelled a hunk of dirt onto his face. As hard as I tried to keep it in, a disgusting spurt of cheap laughter escaped as Soupy shovelled more and more dirt on top. We all joined in until the trench was level.

'Mound it right up,' I said. 'S'pose to rain tomorrow, it'll sink the dirt.'

'Genius Gillings,' Roddy said. 'Maybe we put a fucking headstone up and carve his name on it, just in case the cops are too stupid to realise a mound of dirt that long is a grave.'

'Roddy ... it'll sink and look like a grave anyhow. Seen it happen with trenches I've dug with Dad. People make us come back and top 'em back up to ground level before they pay us.'

'Might have to come back and suss it out, next couple of days,' Soupy said. 'All we can do is grab heaps of leaves and sticks and turf 'em round the whole area. They're not going to come checking this deep in the forest, anyway.'

'How would you know?' I asked.

'Meatlips said so. Why would they anyway, less you're thinking of telling someone he's here. Are you, Gillo?'

'Course not, smartarse.'

'Good,' Soupy said.

We all grabbed handfuls of foliage and threw it around the area and rode our bikes home. Surprisingly, I wasn't tired. I'd heard of adrenaline, how it keeps you going. Rex and I snuck through the laundry door. I crept down the passage into my room and just as I was getting out of my dirty clothes, someone tapped on my door. My jeans were around my ankles and I fell over.

'You all right?' Dad asked in a hushed tone as he opened the door. I tried to remain calm. He had no reason to suspect I'd just buried a kid from a few doors down.

'What's going on?'

'Just went out for a piss.'

'Why's the dog in your room? Shit! What's with the mud? Get out Rex. Get out.'

The dog scampered out. Dad gave him a foot in the bum and I heard the flap of the dog-door in the laundry.

'Got no idea what he's been doing,' I said.

'Digging up freekin' bones, probably.'

It was true. Dad actually said that.

CHAPTER 14

An hour later I was attempting to do my Geography homework in my room before school. I took one bite from my cold Vegemite toast. It turned claggy in my mouth, the taste sharp. I chewed and chewed and still, it stayed in mushy clumps, which I forced down so I had something in my stomach. The remainder was flushed down the toilet to avoid Mum's questioning. To make everything seem in place, I walked the three blocks to the Ackley Street bus stop with Rex. Things had to look normal. I could catch the bus from my street from now on, but that would mean walking past Debono's house and although I didn't know it at the time, I would never walk or ride my bike past that house again. Whenever I drove past in a car or on the bus, I shut my eyes.

Our blue school bus rounded the corner. I hopped on and luckily found a seat on my own behind Danny Corbell, a kid from Debono's grade.

Half way to school, I worked up the courage to lean forward and ask, 'Did you hear about Debono running away on the weekend?'

'Nuh.'

'Soupy swung past my joint earlier this morning while on his paper round. Reckons everyone's talking about it.'

'Nuthin' surprises me with that loony,' he said and as easy as that I'd sewn the first seeds of rumour into the ears of our school. Word got back to me at recess. Someone asked me if I knew anything because I lived in his street. Debono was a popular kid for all the wrong reasons. During that recess I wandered as close as I could to the car park, wondering if Mr. Debono's brown Falcon was there. It wasn't, still I had to check the car park again and again all through lunchtime, too. I stomached half a bunch of grapes and tossed my sandwiches. About fifteen minutes before the bell was due to be sounded to end lunch, I was in the line-up on the handball court waiting for my turn, when a police car drove into the school.

I walked away from the line as quickly as I could to check out the car. The officers paid no attention to either me, or any of the other kids who crowded around to watch. I wondered if they already knew the kid they were looking for. *Me!* Had one of the others broken already? Cudgy. After all we'd been through the night before.

I couldn't run. The school was bordered by farmland on three sides and the Cape Road to the front. I thought of hiding somewhere in the school, maybe in the sabbatical, but that meant big trouble to be caught in there. Instead, it felt like a magnet was drawing me to follow them in through the corridor. The two officers, fully uniformed, guns and all, stood waiting at the office counter. Brother Hobbins greeted them as I walked past rapidly heading for the nearest exit.

'Excuse me officers,' I heard Brother Hobbins say. 'Gillings!' Oh no. Cudgy had squealed. A sense of relief hit me, mixed with the dread of being caught. I froze, glaring at their badges, then their guns and handcuffs. Both officers had huge chests. 'Gillings. What are you doing in the corridor?'

I faced Brother Hobbins.

'You know you are not allowed in the corridor through lunch.' He checked his watch. 'See me five minutes before class. Now go.'

I'd forgotten all about the rule that we weren't allowed in the corridor through lunch unless we had a valid reason – simply because it was about the only rule I'd never broken. It was totally out of character for me to be anywhere near a classroom when I didn't have to be.

'Yes sir.' I hurried out the door. The cops had heard my name and said nothing.

That night the bus talk was alive. *"Cops were after Debono. He's pissed off. Runaway. Beaten someone up. Been busted shoplifting again."*

Hobbins only gave me a lecture for being in the corridor, but for not completing my homework, I received a half an hour's detention and just made it in time for the late bus. Otherwise I'd have had to walk. I went straight home. Mum greeted me at the door with a worried look on her face.

'Honey, come in.' I detected the caution in her voice, she made me feel like a stranger. She'd never told me to come into my own house before. For the first time in my life it didn't feel like home and momentarily, I didn't feel like her son. I walked to the lounge room and sat on the couch without saying anything, without even looking at her. She had to know by now. My knees trembled.

'Honey, Mr. Debono came up today. He wants to know if we've seen Tony. He didn't come home last night. Were you at the quarry on the weekend with your friends?'

I swallowed. Nothing passed the lump in my dry throat. 'No. Heard he ran away.'

'Who told you that?'

'Kids at school. He also told Soupy he planned to knick off a couple of weeks ago.'

'Why would he tell Soupy—'

She corrected herself.

'—Glenn anything? That kid couldn't keep a secret for the life of him.' I knew she didn't approve of Soupy, but she wouldn't dare tell me who my friends should be anymore, like she tried to do in my younger years.

'Wouldn't have a clue. It's all over town. Everyone knows he's run away.'

'Well I really hope that's all this is. His father and mother are very very worried. Does he still pick on you at school, or is that all over now? Is that why you ride your bike sometimes?'

'No, he's fine.' Hunger pains gripped me. I wanted to make a sandwich and get away from the questions. She had this knack of knowing when things were wrong, then I realised the kitchen wasn't the place to get away from her. I also had to see the other guys, meaning I'd have to buy something at the shops even though I hated wasting pocket money when there was food in the cupboard. I changed out of uniform and as I was leaving, I heard Mum on the phone. I knew she was talking to Mr Debono so I got out of there and jumped on my bike. Rex followed me down to Wundowie Street, the main street in town. Cudgy, Roddy and Meatlips were huddled around the Defender machine inside the pinball shop, watching Soupy trying to clock Defender again. I bought a Chiko Roll and wandered over.

'How'd it go at St Peds today?' Meatlips asked. 'All cool?'

'Yeah, cops come but everyone thinks he's just pissed off.'

'Soon as I got here from school another kid told me the same thing, 'Meatlips said. 'Yous done all right. But we also got another problem, Gillo.'

'What's that?'

'He's not deep enough,' Soupy said, concentrating hard on trying to keep his rocket ship alive on the screen. He only had one spare life left.

'What do you mean? He's heaps deep enough.' I looked around, making sure we weren't overheard by other kids, the ones not discussing a buried body. They all seemed busy on other machines or talking, huddled around in their clicky little groups, like us.

'No way,' Meatlips said.

'Where the hell were you last night, anyway?'

'Yeah ... nah. It was best I didn't come, Gillo. But four foot's nowhere near deep enough. Gotta be down at least six foot.'

Surely he wasn't suggesting we go back tonight.

'What about it? We can't go back. What if we get busted?'

'Won't happen. Don't panic. Cops and everyone think he's run away. No one knows he's dead.'

'How would you know?' None of the others had asked any questions, they simply listened. I figured they'd already discussed this amongst themselves at their school.

'Has to be done tonight,' Soupy said.

'What's gotta be done?'

'Yous have to put him deeper,' Meatlips said.

'Serious? Guys, come on.' Another sleepless night! I'd been okay at school and hadn't fallen asleep in class. But I couldn't go through it all again.

'We're all in,' Cudgy said. 'What about you?'

'Guess I have to be.'

*****

Despite the thought of another long night ahead, this time I wanted to do the job properly. So when Dad came inside just before dinner, I went back out and grabbed the crowbar from his ute and slung it over the back fence into the long grass. It would get through clay, no problem at all and Dad once told me the crowbar was six feet tall. Perfect.

They say twenty-four hours makes a difference. What a difference. If I could've taken the last twenty-four hours back, I'd have told them everything last night when I should have. Now we were eating dinner again as a family and there was no way known I could say anything. Mum cooked chops and veggies and mash. The mash slid down easily. Greens tasted like poison and I wrapped most of them in my hanky when no one was watching. I used to love veggies. I chewed the chops as much as I could, then slipped the meat into my hand and under the table to Rex. I couldn't stomach meat.

I went to my room shortly after dinner, set my alarm and dozed off once only to be shattered awake by a nasty dream. Debono, his evil grin, his earring sparkling in my nightmare, larger than the ear it pierced. I remembered a judge. A gavel slammed down. I could still hear it ringing in my subconscious ears when I sat upright. Awake.

My eyes burst open and I looked at the time on my digital clock, hoping it was at least ten. Seven forty-five, only twenty minutes had passed. I picked up my book and began to read, the words bumped into each other and wouldn't clear up. The book was The Shining by a dude named Stephen King, that didn't help either. I had to find something to do. I thought about putting on some music but I knew that would send me back to sleep. I didn't want to go there, the dream was waiting for me to finish it. I also feared sleeping through my alarm, so I reached down beside my bed and found the box my portable tape deck had been packed in. I fumbled around inside and pulled out the bubble wrap and began popping the air from each circle. I got bored with going down the lines, so I went random, criss crossing, selecting bubbles from any line, until I entertained myself by trying to find the last remaining pockets, providing cheap satisfaction in the mind-numbing challenge to find more air pockets with each pop in the darkness. I had to prize my eyelids open several times until finally, it came time to sneak out once again, armed with the Aerogard.

With the crow bar held in one hand and the pointed tip skilfully resting on the handlebars, I managed to steer my bike along the track on top of the creek. If I stacked in the dark, the heavy bar could do me some real damage. Eventually I got the hang of it and met the others at the quarry gates. Soupy and Cudgy had shovels. Roddy held a pick. Rex raced ahead to the gravesite. He knew exactly where we were heading and began scratching at the grave before we even stopped on our bikes.

We dug him up easily, laid him face down with a jumper over his head and began digging. Pick and crowbar, then pick and shovel, chipping away at the hard dirt. I was not so scared this time and didn't scour the bush as much with my torch. We got the job done in less than two hours and by three thirty we had him six feet under and backfilled, packing the dirt down as we went with bracken and leaves spread nicely on top when we finished. Rex and I were in bed by just after four o'clock. I shut my eyes and concentrated hard on sleep. My legs and arms felt like they were filled with lead. Sleep didn't come, but six o'clock and sunlight both did. Homework time.

CHAPTER 15

Tuesday was a quiet day, a strange day. I guess all my days were doomed to be strange from now on. The police came to our school again, this time detectives in dark suits driving an unmarked blue Falcon. After school, two police cars were at the Debonos house. A marked car and the detectives' car I'd seen at school earlier.

I raced down to the pinnies to tell the guys. We hung out on the bench seat in front of the shop where no one could hear us talking. 'Cops came to school again. They're at the Debonos, now. You still reckon they're buying it?'

'Shit yeah,' Meatlips said. 'They've got no reason to think otherwise.'

'Bike's all stripped down,' Roddy said.

'Better not try and sell the parts,' I warned. 'We'll get busted for sure.'

Roddy's face twisted into his tired – *what do you take me for* – look. 'What the fuck Gillings … course not.'

I doubted him, but didn't question it again, to my peril. 'We gotta do anything tonight?' I asked Meatlips.

'Sleep.'

Finally. My body was sore all over and sapped of energy. I'd even thought about sleeping when I got home from school, but the safest place for me was down here, away from Mum. I figured I'd crash tonight like a lead balloon.

My dad's ute pulled up. Soupy had a smoke in his hands and I wished he'd put it out but instead he took a deep drag, showing off as my dad came over.

'Hi boys.'

'Hey Mr. G.,' they all replied.

He sighed and eyeballed each of us, then settled on me. 'Time to come home, mate.'

'It's only early.'

'Just … come on, let's go.'

'All right, see you there.'

'No mate, jump in. Chuck your bike in the back.'

I looked at the other guys. Something was happening, although we had no idea what. Then Dad gave a heavy sigh.

'Listen fellas. It's only fair to warn you the police are at our house and they will come and see you all eventually, probably tonight. They know you all ride in the quarry and it's pretty sad what's happened. They just want to know if you saw Tony Debono last Sunday.'

'Isn't he s'posed to have run away?' Soupy asked.

Dad stood with hands on hips, drew a long breath and shook his head a little. 'No one knows.'

'Sometimes he's down the quarry, didn't see him at all last weekend,' Meatlips said. The lie rolled off his tongue easily. 'We were there after lunch, but didn't stay long.'

Dad gave us a sorry look. 'The police are going to ask if you were riding there.' His gaze fell on me. 'Your mother's gonna hit the roof. You told her you'd been here at the shops last Sunday afternoon.'

'Yeah well it's easier Dad, you know. She doesn't like me riding. I'll just say the truth … was at the quarry with the guys. Won't say I was riding.'

'Suppose so. Guess it sounds a little better,'

That was our story anyway. Meatlips had told us not to say anything else and that's all I told the detectives at my house. They were the same two men who came to my school. Mum had already made a pot of tea and when she introduced the officers, my clouded mind tried to remember their names moments afterwards and failed. Other than that, I passed their questioning with ease. One was Scottish. The other did the talking. They stayed for about ten minutes, sipped tea and asked their questions.

'Have you seen him?'

'No.'

'Does he ride down the quarry?'

'Yes.'

'Did you see him at the quarry last Sunday?'

'No.'

'Who were you with?'

I told them and gave them a description of his motorbike, which I assumed they already had. They didn't check our garage, meaning they wouldn't check Roddy's either because they had no reason to. No reason at all I convinced myself. Earlier in the car on the way home with Dad, I'd been shitting myself. Now as I watched their car drive away I couldn't believe how easy it was. We were in the clear.

After dinner Mum laid down the law. 'I'll be driving you boys to and from school from now on.'

'What … why?' I asked, but I knew her reasoning. 'I can catch the bus.'

'You haven't caught the bus for a while.'

'Caught it this week. Sometimes I ride but—' I was about to say I don't need to ride anymore, but I stopped myself short.

Mum read my mind. 'You've caught the bus the last couple of mornings. Why have you stopped riding your new bike?'

'Can't be bothered. Mum, really it's fine … I'll catch the bus. I'll even catch it from our street.'

'Well, all right then but I don't want you boys going out after school for a while.'

What? I couldn't believe it.

'Can't I play in the street?' Tommy asked.

'No dear. I really want you to stay inside, or in the back yard. Just for the time being.'

'You're kidding?' I said.

'No honey.'

'But I meet the other guys—'

'Jack. Please.' She flicked a glance at Tommy and gave a pleading look. 'Please bear with me.' Obviously she believed something had happened and she wanted to protect Tommy.

That wasn't fair on me. I was five years older than Tommy and had to keep in contact with the others to find out what was going on. I was effectively grounded. What next? I wanted to tell her there was no bad man getting around town.

I'M RESPONSIBLE MUM, I longed to shout.

I decided to test her out. 'He's just run away, Mum.'

'Yeah Mum, that's what I heard too,' Tommy said.

'I hope so boys … I really do.' With her big finger, she brushed away tears forming in the bottom of her eyes.

I turned to Tommy. 'Mate, can you shove off for a minute?'

He gave me a quizzical look. Mum nodded and he disappeared into the lounge room.

I spoke as firmly as I dared. 'I'm not being grounded, Mum. You haven't grounded me since I was twelve and … I'm not in any trouble.'

'I'm not grounding you and this is not about you being in trouble—'

'He's run away, he told us he was going to … ages ago, and he told other kids too.'

'Jack, honey, I … I have to say something to you.' She put on a brave face and wiped the corner of her left eye again. 'I don't believe the police think he's run away.'

I opened my mouth to say something but she scrunched her eyes and held her palm up to stop me talking again. 'I know you're older now, but you still must do as you're told. I need you to stay inside with Tommy … please. At least until—' She paused; I think she summoned up a batch of courage. 'At least until he's found.'

What had I done to her? 'Can I catch the bus, at least?'

She twisted her lips in her normal gesture of thought, then she pointed her finger. 'As long as you catch it from our street and as long as you come straight home. No ifs or buts.'

I stormed off to my room, slumped on my bed and closed my eyes in desperate need of sleep, but anger kept me awake. Ten minutes later I heard a knock at my door.

'Jack. You wanna play draughts with me?' Tommy said.

'Piss off, Tommy.' When I heard him run back down the hall, I hoped he wasn't crying. I felt so bad, blaming him for me being grounded and yet it was entirely my fault, not his. I'd never said anything like that to him before and he was a great kid who didn't deserve it. Neither did my oldies, but telling them everything would certainly mean I'd be sent to juvy, and that would shatter them just as much. Maybe more if that was possible. I pictured the walls of juvy, pale with dim lights like on Prisoner, a TV show Mum watched. The other kids inside would be like those women in the show, moping about and blueing with each other all day long. I didn't want to be like that. Roddy was right for once in his pathetic life. I had to weigh up whether I wanted my life to change forever and if I told my parents everything, it would still do nothing for Debono. Nothing could bring him back. We had done what we'd done, and our only choice was to stick together.

There was another knock at the door. 'Jack, did you say something to Tommy?'

'Sorry, Mum. I'll apologise.'

'Make sure you do ... and look after him please. Your father and I are going down the road to see the Debonos ... to offer some support.'

I watched them through my window as they disappeared down the driveway, holding hands. I went straight out through the laundry door to the shed and did something I'd never done before. I pinched two of Dad's stubbies, went down to the creek bed and sat on the edge of the embankment, alone. Rex and Tommy were soon by my side.

*****

That night in bed, exhaustion and the two beers made sure I fell asleep. The gavel slammed down in my dream, echoing out the door of the courtroom into the halls of justice.

"I FIND THE BUSHMORE KILLERS CLUB GUILTY OF MURDER IN THE FIRST DEGREE," yelled the judge.

"MOTOCROSS CLUB. MOTOCROSS CLUB. BUSHMORE MOTOCROSS CLUB," screamed the four of us at the tops of our voices at the judge, who already had his back to us and was leaving through a side, wood-panelled door.

Debono stood in the dock, sniggering away and pointing to the chain of bruising on his neck. Voices jeered from behind. I wanted Meatlips here. He was nowhere. Hands reached out, grappling our arms.

'Jack. Jack. Wake up. Wake up, Jack.'

Fingers gripped my biceps. I woke to cold sweat over my skin.

'Jack, are you all right?' I recognised my father's voice.

The door was open. Faint light entered from the passage and when I made out his face in the semi darkness, I realised I was in my room. Terrified.

CHAPTER 16

Choppers came on Wednesday, two of them at first. We heard the distant thudding of rotors in the sky. Before school, kids were lined against the fence watching through the diamond shapes in the wire as they hovered about like dragonflies over the vicinity of the quarry. 'They're got bears in the air,' an excited kid called out, ringing a line from the trucking movie, Convoy. Everyone laughed, except me. None of my schoolmates knew the cops had visited my house, and like the rest of them, I was in awe of what was going on. Although, mine was a different type of awe. That fair dinkum packing darkies type of awe, wondering why the hell they were over the quarry.

Normally we said prayers in class, but at eight forty, Father Frost and Brother Hobbins assembled the entire school in the quadrangle area, a bitumen section of the playground used for basketball in front of the main building. They led us all in prayer for the safe return of Debono. I stood there, head down eyes up, studying the kids in front of me. All in neat rows muttering prayers. I had a headache and reckoned it was from all the guilt and regret piling up. But the more time passed, the more I realised there was no turning back. As I peered at the backs of their heads, I knew I'd been right all along about how useless prayers were. In fifteen years of life, I'd only ever been told what God could do. All tell and no show. I'd never seen any evidence of God raising a hand to help anyone. Truth was, he couldn't help Debono because he was under a whole lot of forest and the only person who could help me, and save me from juvenile prison, was me. Not prayer. Not God.

Once when I was young, Mum had gone away overnight and Dad had tucked me in. I said my prayers in bed and he had asked me why.

'Cause Mum says I should pray to God every night.'

'Your mother says she has to pray for her sins in the church or in the confessional. Reckons the message can only be delivered through the priest, and then onto God.'

'Yeah, that's true,' I had said. 'But what's wrong with that?'

'My point is,' my father replied, 'you seem to be talking to God now. Why can't your mum just pray at home like you and save me a truckload of cash.'

I remember that conversation well. I think it was something Dad found easier to say to me when Mum wasn't around, and he definitely would not have said it to her face. He was drunk at the time too. But it was one of the few things about religion that has ever made any sense to me and soon after, I asked Mum if I could stop going to church because I didn't need a priest to hook me up to God. She asked me where I got that information from and Dad got into strife over that one.

Now I found myself wondering what the hell would prayer do for someone who was not only dead, but buried twice. Classes went slow. Helicopters tapped away inside my head and I struggled to stay awake, stretching my eyelids open. I even had a crazy thought of propping them up with five-cent coins because I was so shit-scared of nodding off. I also got in strife for biting my nails in class, I hadn't done that for years and didn't realise I was even doing it until I was told off the first time. That same nightmare returned several times during the previous night. Each time I woke, I'd broken out in sweat, panicking, wondering where I was. Then felt overwhelming relief when I discovered I was safe in my room. I'd spent the dark, early morning hours staring at the ceiling, contemplating my bleak future. Snapping myself out of small, difficult patches of sleep so the dream wouldn't haunt me. No way could I risk that nightmare happening in class.

I kept away from my schoolmates, content to be on my own through recess and lunch, away from the rumours of Debono's fate. After school I broke the deal I'd made with Mum and got off the bus in the middle of town. The urge to find out the events of the day was too strong. I'd have to wear Mum's wrath when I got home. I walked past the church, the cop station and the pub on my way to the shops. Every telephone pole I passed had a missing persons notice with Debono's face. After the first two, I shied away from the others. My dead-tired mind tried to blank them back to meaningless sheets of paper as best I could.

The boys were out the front of the pinnies.

'You heard what's going on?' Roddy asked. His eyes danced around like we were being spied upon, or listened to by secret microphones.

'Nope, but saw the choppers from school.'

'News and cops,' Roddy said. 'Swarming over the quarry all day. Pissed off from school the minute I saw 'em, went straight down there. Everything's locked up. Cops have chained the gates … put guards on it. Had to sneak under the fence and watch from the clubhouse.'

'What'd you see … and what could they find anyway?'

Roddy gave me his stupid look. I'd seen it many times over the years.

'Tell him,' Meatlips said.

I stared back. 'Tell me what?'

Roddy flicked his eyes away, looking for spies again, then eyeballed me. 'Dumped some parts in there.'

'What?' Then it hit me. The bike. 'Oh, you fucking dumb ass.' I wanted to wring his fat neck, wanted to see his head squirt like a giant pimple. 'How could you be so stupid? What parts?'

Roddy shrugged like he didn't have a care in the world. 'Engine, gearbox … don't worry, they'll sink in the mud. Told ya! I watched 'em search the trees n' shit. Not the water.'

I felt a cold tingle inside my chest. 'And the frame?'

Roddy glanced around at the others.

'Oh Christ … no Roddy. Serial numbers. Might as well have chucked his fuckin' body in there too.'

'Ahhh, no worries Gillings. Filed 'em all down, they can't check nothing.'

'Don't worry you reckon. And you think they're not going to know it's from his bike.'

'Stop panicking Gillings, you're worrying like an old mole at a christening.' He laughed but not convincingly. None of the others laughed either and I certainly couldn't see the funny side.

'Uncle Dan always says that.'

I glared at him. He was such a fucking idiot.

Roddy kept going. 'Gimme a break. While you guys were in nodd last night, I was out covering our arses. Wiped everything down, no way'd I leave any prints. Where the fuck else was I going to chuck it? No way was I gonna bury that stuff at my joint. Cops came to my house too, you know.'

'They came to all of our houses,' Soupy said. 'Just asking the same questions … but—'

I shook my head in disbelief. 'What about the rest of it?'

'Still in my shed. Bins go out tonight.' Roddy said. 'I'll keep the bits that could have come off any bike.'

Pain rose behind my forehead again. *Self-inflicted* was the term my dad would have used. Often, when talking politics I'd heard him say the reason why our nation's finances were so stuffed up, was because we elected numbskulls straight out of university who had no idea of what a real job was, or how to run a business. Then we'd allow them to run a whole country. He'd go on to say it was self-inflicted because we were the idiot plebs who voted them in.

Now I totally realised what he meant. Our problem was self-inflicted too. We left the stupidest one amongst us in charge of the most crucial piece of evidence that could bring all of our

PETER EDWARDS

lies crashing down on us. He'd dumped it exactly where we told him not to, and now all we had to do was wait until they announced that Debono's motorbike had been found in the quarry.

I rubbed my temples to stop them throbbing. 'Get rid of it all. Just get rid of the lot, for fuck's sake.'

'Stop stressin', Gillo,' Meatlips said. 'Roddy's right. Reckon the parts 'll sink in the mud. They can't know who turfed 'em in there anyway, even if they do find out they're off his bike.'

'And how do you know there's mud in the bottom of the quarry? No one even knows how deep it is.'

'Gotta be chockers full of mud,' Cudgy said. 'Water's been there for donkey's years.'

I ignored him. 'What do we do about this?'

Meatlips shrugged. 'Fuck all. Cops obviously reckon he's been murdered or kidnapped … both probably. Just act normal. They won't come back to talk to us again. Can't prove shit.'

Act normal, I thought. How could I act normal? Someone somewhere had decided Debono was dead. Now all they had to do was find out who killed him.

CHAPTER 17

Soon after, Mum's car pulled up in front of the shops. She pointed to the passenger side, stabbing the air, screwing her face up. I turned to the guys. 'I'm up shit creek just for being here.'

'Sucks having a Catholic mum ... hey,' Roddy said with a huge grin.

In theory I almost agreed with him, but said, 'She's no fuckin' alco like yours.'

'Least I do what I want—'

'Shut up yous two,' Meatlips said. 'We'll be at your joint soon, Gillo. Meet us out front.'

'That's if that dragon *lets* ya out,' Roddy said.

I wanted to wipe that stupid grin away with my fist, but ignored him and headed to Mum's car for the impending argument. Also, I wondered why they wanted to come to my house.

Mum didn't say a word until we got around the corner.

'Honey. I found a pair of jeans down the creek behind our house. They're yours. Have you been crook lately?'

Shit.

What was she doing down at the creek? She never went there. I'd forgotten all about the jeans.

'Yeah ... just something I ate ... last week.'

'Why didn't you tell me? I'd 've washed them for you.'

'Mum ... just threw up, that's it. They were torn anyway.' I was wondering if they'd all searched the creek during the day and if so, why? Why didn't they believe he'd run away?

'Were you drinking? Don't you lie to me now.'

'No Mum.'

'If you're lying to me—' She served up this suspicious look, then gave up on that and unloaded on me for not coming home after school. She was angry and kept paying out until we pulled into the driveway.

I was spitting chips. I wanted to tell her *where to go,* but neither had the guts or the real want to do it. I thought about saying it though, at least a half a dozen times while she was going off, but I also didn't want Roddy to have his moment once I told him.

As we drove up the driveway, I noticed a large three sided missing persons billboard had been erected in the Debono's front yard, higher than the fence – like a real estate agent's *for sale* sign. One side faced the other end of the street, another side faced the road and the third side faced our house at a forty-five degree angle, complete with Debono's school picture, grinning back.

Now I knew they'd been searching the creek for sure. Why? Were they looking for a body? Mum warned me not to leave the house. I went straight to my room and slammed the door shut. I hated being caged at home after school and thought of climbing out my window, but decided to not upset her anymore. Plus, the guys were coming to my house, anyway. Tommy knocked, breaking my angry mood. 'Can we play draughts, Jack?'

'Why not.' He entered with a broad grin, carrying a board with the pieces all set up. On purpose I made a few bad moves in the first game and he slaughtered me. Same thing happened in the second game. I felt glad to make up for swearing at him last night. We began setting up the third game when I heard a knock at the front door, followed by voices. Tommy and I went out to find the boys talking to Mum.

'He's not allowed out for the time being,' she said.

'We'll be sitting out front. Calm down Mum.' I pushed my way past without waiting for a reply.

'Don't go past the gate.'

We walked down the driveway.

'You're old lady's so strict, bet you gotta ask permission to cut a fart in the dunny,' Soupy said, lighting a cigarette.

'Not fuckin' wrong,' I said. 'Why'd you light up? Can't you wait till we get out the front?'

'She's not *my* mum.'

'Just tell her to fuck off,' Roddy said.

I spun on him with a raised fist. 'So help me Roddy … you ever say that to me again and I'll smash you deeper than—' *Debono,* I was about to say but stopped and glanced at the front door. Thank God Mum was gone. Rex snarled at Roddy. We stood chest to chest. He was a little taller and much heavier. I didn't care. I had my dog. 'I swear Roddy. Ever say that to me again, I'll thump you something shocking. Only reason you can say that to your old lady is cause—', I wanted to say she's a bitch of a woman but held off, '—is cause she couldn't give a shit about you. Can tell that by what she feeds you.' That felt much better than throwing a punch.

He stared at me through steely eyes. 'Bit touchy, Gillings … better watch ya lip. Might fatten it up for ya.'

'Go'n try. I dare ya. I'll kick your fat arse—'

Meatlips placed a palm between us. 'Guys, come on. Take a look.'

I moved away from Roddy and watched as the unmarked Falcon turned the far corner. The two detectives glared at us as they passed by, like we were beneath a microscope lens in science class. We hurried to the front fence as they pulled up at Debono's house and walked through the gate. The Scottish cop poised at the sign, eyeballing us. I'd forgotten his name but Roddy said, 'Bottomly. I hated that pig the second I laid eyes on him.'

'Me too,' Cudgy said as Detective Bottomly followed his partner to the door.

'What's that other arsehole's name?' I asked.

'Hayden,' Cudgy said.

'What do you reckon they're doing?' It was day four and he surprised me that he was still holding his nerve, but of course it was way too late for even him to weaken and lag us in.

'Who knows,' Soupy said.

'They're just letting his pairs know the progress of the investigation,' Meatlips said, 'or lack of it. If they've found him and dug him up ... wouldn't be wearing suits, would they?'

That didn't sound logical, but I let it ride. It also became obvious to me that Meatlips expected the cops to be at Debono's house tonight and he wanted to keep an eye on them, although I had no idea what he thought we could possibly gain by doing this.

'How do you know they ain't found him yet?' Cudgy said, with his typical whimpering voice.

'They'll never find him, and they don't know jack-shit,' Meatlips said. 'We just gotta watch them.'

'What good 'll that do?' I asked, and also chose not to tell him I thought the creek had been searched today, because nothing could be done about that either.

'You never know what can happen by watching.'

There was absolutely nothing we could learn by watching, but we waited and talked amongst ourselves. The police were still inside when, at five to six Meatlips said, 'News is on. Let's go in.'

We wandered inside. All three major channels led their bulletins with the disappearance of Tony Debono from our town, Bushmore.

Mum sat with us on the couch. We all watched, dumbstruck. The footage showed police divers in the water.

Divers. We were screwed big-time.

Roddy jolted forward, then turned and said, 'Hey watch it,' to Meatlips, who – I think – must have jabbed him in the back.

Roddy. How did I ever get stuck with him for a friend? Was there something other kids saw all those years ago in grade prep or even kindergarten? Did they realise way back then that he was a dud and left him for me? Why didn't I see it too, and what did that say about me? The cops would surely find the bike parts and know they hadn't been in the water for long. Why didn't they believe he'd run away? Seemed logical to everyone else in our town, at least the kids at school believed it.

Mum focused on the telly, even though a commercial had started. Her hand rose to her eyes and she brushed away the beginnings of tears.

'You reckon they'll find him, Mum?' Tommy asked with an eager expression, like this was some story from a Hardy Boys novel.

She studied us all. 'I hope to God they do—'

'You reckon he's been murdered … kidnapped even, Mum?'

She gasped. 'Tommy … no sweety. Of course not.' But I could tell by her sad eyes she didn't believe her own words. She wiped away more tears with the back of her hand. 'Tea's almost ready. You boys 'll have to go.'

'No worries Mrs. G,' Meatlips said, and we all headed for the front door.

'Jack, I'm putting your tea out now, don't go outside please.'

'Just be a minute, Mum.' I followed the guys as they walked their bikes down the driveway in silence. Once we were out of mum's range, I could no longer hold myself back. 'Divers Roddy? You didn't say nuthin' about no divers.'

'I didn't know … couldn't see 'em down in the water.'

The police car was still out the front of the Debono's house. 'You didn't think to take a look, huh? You dump his bike in the water and when you see cops at the quarry, it didn't occur to you to check for divers.' I pressed my brows with my thumb and first two fingers, stretching the skin, tight. Why didn't I listen to my mind when I knew months ago that as

129

mates, we were on our way out? 'What flows through your shit for brains Roddy? What *do* you think about?'

'Don't be a fuckin' smartarse, Gillings. Cops searching the bushes … it's all I could see. How am I s'posed to see 'em in the water from the clubhouse?'

There was no point causing a scene and arguing with Roddy. I turned to the rest of the guys. 'What now?'

'Nuthin',' Soupy replied, butting out his smoke. 'Nuthin' we can do. You saw the news. They found fuck all. Few car bodies, that's it.'

'Cops won't say if they found anything,' I said. 'My old man reckons believe half of half of what they tell you on the news. He says cops do deals with the press all the time about when to leak shit out.'

'Stop being so paranoid, Gillo,' Meatlips said. 'They can't find out nothing—'

'Paranoid!' I seemed to be doing all the thinking here. 'How can I *not* be paranoid? Half his fuckin' bike's down there.' I glared at him, unable to believe his slack attitude.

'You're freaking out too much,' Meatlips said.

I watched them all ride away, seemingly without a care. I had good reason to be freaking out. The outside world was closing in on us. Cops too. I could feel it, sense it. I saw it. Down the street the Debono's gate opened up and the two detectives walked to their car. Bottomly turned and gave me a forceful glare as Dad's ute came around the corner, groaning and squeaking as it bounced over the gutter and up the driveway.

That night we ate dinner in relative silence, for a family who loved to chat at the table. Even Tommy hardly spoke a word. Perhaps he'd worked out for himself Debono wasn't coming back. Kids at his school were obviously talking too.

Mum's brother, Uncle Colin rang that night.

I answered but didn't recognise the voice until he told me who he was. He lived in far North Queensland and hardly ever called. 'Hey knackers, what's going on in that pissy little town of yours?'

'Kid's just run away.'

'Not what the news up here says. Did you know him?'

I ignored the past tense. 'He's in my school, lives down the road.'

'That's no good. Stick your mum on, champ.'

I passed the phone to Mum and went to bed early. My arms and legs barely worked, my neck was so stiff not even my pillow could ease the discomfort.

I shut my eyes and dreamt of police in white uniforms combing through the rubbish tip. Machinery hummed and droned, spreading piles and piles of garbage and stench over open spaces to make the search easier. Seagulls screeched from dark corners. Bottomly held up a green garbage bag and they all searched through the bag with the parts. Bottomly read an envelope with Roddy's address on it. *"We've got those lying little shites now,"* he said as I sat bolt upright, swamped in the now familiar cold dampness of sweat. Darkness surrounded me and I had a solid boner, which always seemed to pop up lately because I was so overtired. My alarm clock displayed nine-fifteen. Only an hour of sleep had passed, but suddenly I'd never felt more alive knowing Roddy was about to make another huge mistake. I listened to the house. The TV in the lounge room was on; Mum and Dad were still awake. I had to contact Roddy to tell him not to dump the rest of the parts in his own bin. Surely he was not that stupid. Surely one of the others would have said something, but I couldn't trust any of those dimwits. I thought about sneaking into my pairs' room to ring Roddy from the extension, but couldn't chance being busted if Dad or Mum picked up the other phone.

I laid still, unable to read, fearing that horror book would bring on more traumatising sleep. My door creaked open, oblong light spilled in. I shut my eyes, rolled over and took a break from staring at the blank ceiling. The door closed with a tender click.

I had to get to Roddy's. Another fifteen nervous minutes passed – one by one – before I snuck out of bed and dressed. I told Rex to stay this time while I worked the screen loose and out the window I went. Seconds later I climbed back in, even quieter and scribbled a note.

MUM I'M FINE. NEEDED SOME AIR. WENT FOR A RIDE.
XXX JACK.

She thought some nutcase was running around town and I couldn't have her believe I'd been taken too. I climbed back out, found my old pushy and took off through the dark streets.

As I pumped the pedals, chilly air sliced the back of my throat, like what happened when a cold was coming on. I hadn't even thought to bring a jumper. As best as I could, I took mental notes of the bins out the front of each house, looking for the plastic ones. The steel bins would make a racket when we put the lids back on, but the lids on the plastic ones only made a quiet suction noise. Most were dark green with light green lids, some were even orange with black lids. Dad reckoned everyone wanted to make a statement nowadays and having orange bins was a cheap way to do it. I especially took note of the full plastic ones. They nearly always split. Some of the bins that were so chockers had splits down both sides and were definitely no good to us.

When I got to Roddy's, the shed lights were on down the back of the house. Kitchen lights, too. His mum and Uncle Dan would be up drinking. I crept quietly toward the shed and when I opened the door, Soupy gasped, knocking the lit end of his smoke against the workbench. Sparks flew, landing on his fingers. He shook them off.

'Nice one dickhead,' Roddy said. 'There's petrol in here. What the hell you doing sneaking up on us like that? Thought it was fuckin' cops.'

'Scared the shit out of me,' Soupy said.

'Sorry guys.' I noticed three bins with the numbers 8, 10 and 17 painted on the sides, and yes, they'd grabbed the steel ones. At least Roddy had thought it through enough to use his neighbours' bins, rather than his own. But after I explained why we couldn't even use the neighbours' bins, they agreed and we decided to dump the parts in random bins around the streets. I told them to only use the plastic ones. We chopped the parts up as small as possible and began our mission, taking different pieces and riding off and dumping them, then returning for more until we emptied all of the evidence from the bins in Roddy's shed. On my last run I was dumping the brake cables three blocks away, when headlights turned the corner. *Cops* rushed into my head and to avoid being seen, I steered over the nature strip into someone's front yard and crashed through a rose bush, cutting my arms and face and neck. What else could go wrong? I hated rose bushes. They always got in the way when Dad and I were working. If we broke one of their precious branches the owners would spin out. Some would even dock us money.

Then the porch light came on and some old guy in white bogcatchers appeared, the barrel of a shotgun protruded into the darkness. I waited in silence with thorns jabbing all over. That was so hard to do. He watched for any sign of movement, then the light switched off and he disappeared. Slowly I hauled my arse up, scratching myself some more.

'What the hell happened to your face?' Soupy asked, when we met back at the shed.

I told him of my mishap and they laughed at my expense. I joined in – a light-hearted moment in a tough week.

'We're both wagging again tomorrow,' Roddy said. 'If you wanna come, be at the clubhouse, first light. Gotta keep an eye on the cops.'

'What's the use?' I felt relieved now, and I'd feel much better once the rubbish was collected. 'You can't stop the cops doing anything and they'll still be guarding the joint too. Don't be so stupid. They'll bust your arses.'

'No chance,' Soupy said. 'Meatlips reckons we just gotta watch. Keep one step ahead in-case they wanna suss us out again.'

I stared at him for long seconds, but didn't argue. He was almost asleep standing up and had to start his paper round before six that morning.

Earlier in the year, Soupy had slept over at my house and we'd snuck out after midnight and pinched a four foot high cement garden stork and lugged it all the way to the train line. We stood it between the tracks like the Road Runner bird. Except this thing didn't run away, it went off like a bomb when the night train hit it. Then Soupy had to get up a few hours later for his paper round. He was so knackered afterwards, he didn't move from the mattress on the floor until after lunch. Roddy would be going out there on his own in the morning, nothing was surer. I pedalled home and climbed through my window, happy to see the note untouched on my side table.

CHAPTER 18

My only good break in the whole week came when the Brothers decided not to give us any more homework for a while, due to the stress put on the school by Debono's disappearance. So I stayed in bed until seven the following morning, Thursday.

'What in God's name has happened to your face?' my mother asked when I came out to breakfast after she'd woken me by thumping on my door. I'd forgotten to check how bad it really was and didn't answer her.

'Jack. Answer me.'

I was dead tired again. My nightmare with Debono and the judge had only returned once the previous night. All I remembered was kind of like jarring myself awake to get out of there. I don't fully know if I did that or not, or whether it was just part of the dream, but I didn't sleep much after that. Still, I had enough wits about me and was able to think on my feet. 'Just scratched myself on some branches ... last night. Down the creek.'

She gave me this hard glare. Her eyes creased up and I knew she was sussing me right out when she passed my cereal. 'Eat up, honey,' she said, cautiously and hurried down the passage.

My mind screamed at me to follow her so I did, after she closed her bedroom door. I listened from the passage.

'I think he's done it on purpose ... get up will you ... get up and take a look at your son.'

'What?' I heard Dad groan.

'Get up you lazy thing and see for yourself. I think he's done it to himself ... like he's crying out for attention or something.'

I heard the sound of my father's heels hitting the floorboards and darted into the bathroom, locking the door. For the first time I saw the scratch marks on my cheeks and neck. I washed myself as much as I could before I had to face him.

The knock came on the bathroom door. 'Jack, open up.'

I let my father in. He looked shagged. Another hangover.

'So you scratched yourself on some bushes, huh?'

'Just went down the creek to sit on my own.'

'Your mother has asked you not to leave the house.'

'Dad, I'm fifteen.'

'She's worried. Tony was—'

He pulled himself up, scratching his head.

'—is sixteen. Man, I gotta get off the piss, feel like shit warmed up. Please do as she asks. It's a tough time for everyone. You okay, mate?'

We stood facing each other, him deprived of fluids, me deprived of sleep once again. On mornings like this he'd get up and drink almost a whole bottle of juice or soft drink, whatever his hand found first in the fridge. His cheeks were saggy and he had a face full of whiskers and the bags under his eyes were dark. All of a sudden he looked older. *We killed Debono;* I longed to tell him but instead, I said, 'Yeah ... I'm good.'

'Mum's doing it hard ... she thinks—'

He raked his hands through his hair.

'—she thinks something's happened. Me—'

He shrugged.

'—reckon he's just run away. That's all this is mate, and ... well, I dunno ... stacks of rumours and crap floating around. Hey, listen. Noticed a couple a beers missing the other day.'

'Took em' down the creek ... sorry.'

He nodded. 'That's all right, mate. You okay … I mean … you stressed out about all this, or anything?'

My fucking oath, were the first words to spring into my head but what came out was, 'Nah, I'm fine, really … reckon he's just pissed off too … Melbourne maybe.'

'Who knows?' He rubbed my shoulder. 'Next time you pinch a beer, let me know. Rather know what you're up to … better than having you sneak around behind my back.' He huffed out a small laugh. 'Never know. Might even join you next time. Not one to miss out, eh.'

We both gave uneasy chuckles. 'Tell me you didn't do that shit to your face, this isn't an attention thing is it?'

'No, Dad.'

'I'd like to think there's nothing you can't tell me … is there?'

Oh Christ. Don't ask that. 'Course not.' I shrugged it off.

'Just do as your mother asks. Please, mate.'

'I'm not putting up with being grounded just cause some stupid kid's run away.'

'All right … I'll talk to her. Hop out. Let me take a shit.' He was either satisfied or relieved the man to man was over. He was never good at that stuff, especially in such a hungover state, so I went back out to finish what I could of my soggy breakfast.

When I left for school, I noticed Mum peeking through the blinds to make sure I caught the bus from our street. I walked up toward the corner, away from that sign. Debono's eyes stabbed me in the back. Even though there was no bus stop down that end, George stopped when I waved him down. I sat on my own, listening in to the chatter of the other kids. Debono was on everyone's lips. When the bell rang for school, Brother Hobbins announced over the loud speaker we were to line up again for prayer. More useless prayers. Fruitless words to ward off our common denominator, death.

Was this going to be a ritual torture every day? Would getting away with this be my curse?

CHAPTER 19

Dad did speak to Mum because that afternoon she let me out on the condition I only went down the main street. Roddy told us he'd be the first kid from Bushmore to make prime time news. He bragged about how he was filmed being led out of the quarry. Soupy had slept in of course, even missed his paper round and we all laughed at Roddy's antics. He thought it rather cool that the cops took him home. Then they had to drive him to school when they saw his mother crashed out on the couch.

That afternoon a media presence hung over our town, the likes we'd never imagined. Cars clogged the parking spaces in the main street, mostly outside the pub. Dad's ute was also there, along with the cars of just about every other worker in town.

On the poster nailed to the telephone pole out the front of the shops, some kid had drawn black rings around Debono's eyes and hooks around his ears, so it looked like he wore glasses. They'd also drawn a big cock between the glasses, rising from his forehead. That was the first time I think I really felt totally sorry for him, but there was nothing I could do except tear it down, which I did. Up on the next block we saw Media cars from every T.V. station, along with newspaper reporters out the front of the police station, all huddled together beneath the spread of a large pine.

'Might be a press conference,' Meatlips said.

The sun was still high above the treetops in the west as we rode up to the police station and propped on our bikes in the roadside gravel to watch. The detectives' car was parked in the side alley between the police station and the theatre, but there was also activity over the road at our church. A special Mass had been organised for seven thirty that evening.

Out the front, Father Frost chatted to a short, half bald guy in a brown turtleneck jumper. They appeared to be arguing. Father shook his head and held out his hands in a – *what can I do* – type of gesture, as another one of the media crews carried camera gear into the church. Leads of wiring led out the door, but my attention was drawn to the high pitched, clinking sound of steel pegs being hammered into the ground. Mr. Wendsley – the old man whose garden Soupy and Debono had fought in – appeared to be roping off sections of the grassed area on either side of the concrete path in front of the church. I looked back to the bald man who motioned with his head and wandered over to his white news van. Father Frost followed. I couldn't see what happened once they got to the car, but Father tucked something in his top pocket. I think it was cash. They shook hands.

Voices came from behind us. Heaps of locals were walking up from the shopping strip towards the police station. Some – including my dad – were holding pots of beer. They stopped at the front of the church to watch the press conference.

Detective Bottomly emerged, flanked by two uniformed officers and his partner, Detective Hayden. We rode our bikes closer as Bottomly addressed the media, speaking slowly in his Scottish accent.

One of the uniformed cops saw us and walked around behind the pack of reporters. 'Hey fellas,' he said, 'this is a media conference, can you please move along to the other side of the road? Give us a bit of space, you know.'

'You can't stop us being here,' Soupy said.

I was shocked he would stand up to an officer like that. The guy had been polite, after all.

'Tell you what, smartarse. How about you kids move along and I won't take those cigarettes in your top pocket off you. Deal?'

'My pairs let me smoke … you can't do stuff all.'

I couldn't believe Soupy was challenging a cop like that, after what we'd been through all week. All of a sudden a hundred mouths seemed to fire a hundred questions. Together we looked up, ignoring the cop.

'Has Tony Debono been murdered—?'

'Abducted—?'

'Do you believe the rumours he's run away, Detective Bottomly?'

'I repeat,' Bottomly said in a loud voice, hands raised, 'no more questions.'

He turned and walked back into the building amidst yelling reporters and flashing cameras.

We rode off – four killers and Meatlips, an accessory after the fact – in front of the crowd who went back to doing what they'd been doing minutes ago. The pub was filled again within seconds.

'It's almost six,' Meatlips said. 'News 'll be on in a minute.'

The pub was the only place in the street with a telly, (other than the pizza shop and we'd have to buy something if we were to sit in there) so we wandered over to the pub, cupped our hands against the windows and tried to see the screen.

'My old man's in there,' Soupy said. 'Yours too, Gillo. Let's go in.'

'We can't just walk in there,' Cudgy said.

'You can stay out here,' Soupy said and in he went. We all slipped through the door behind him. I'd never walked in on my own before and felt like I grew a little older the instant I stepped inside. I peered around for Dad but couldn't find him through the jam-packed mass of bodies. No one seemed to notice us and everyone shut up when the urgent, dramatic news bulletin music – which Dad always reckoned was designed to make us normal plebs feel alarmed – started up.

We stared up at the screen through the cigarette smoke. Bushmore had been bumped off the headline story by an I.R.A bombing in Ulster, then came our turn.

'And now,' Brian, the newsreader said, 'to the mysterious disappearance of a young boy in the southwestern Victorian town of Bushmore that has gripped the nation's attention. Sixteen-year-old Tony Debono has not been seen since he left the family home on Sunday afternoon to go trail bike riding. Police are focusing their investigation on an abandoned quarry, southeast of the town. Brendan Deacon reports.'

Roddy wore an eager, expectant grin from ear to ear, waiting for his appearance. Cameras from overhead choppers showed the green slime being pumped out through the wire fence into the bush. We saw footage of a crane hauling out a car body from the mud and lines of police and volunteers in orange fire fighting overalls combing through nearby paddocks. As a member of the Country Fire Authority, Dad would have been amongst them. The reporter signed off from the press conference in front of the police station.

The line searching concerned me the most, even though they were checking paddocks a long way from Denhams Creek. Despite the report saying they hadn't found any trace of Debono, sooner or later they'd be searching the bush.

When our story finished (that's what my warped mind called it at the time, *our story*) we all turned to Roddy. His shoulders slumped, his face couldn't hide his embarrassment.

'You got the chop, Roddy,' I said, grinning.

'Screw you guys.' He stormed out of the pub and we all laughed at him before I made my way to the bar.

'Kid's been murdered for sure,' someone said as I slipped my way through to find Dad drinking with Bruce and Lenny Botwin. All three were dressed in fire fighting overalls.

'Hey mate,' he said. 'Mum let you out?'

'She can't treat me like a kid no more.'

'I know.'

'Whatever you said … thanks.'

'Just stop arguing with her, will ya. This is a hard time for everyone and your mother feels it more than most. She has her reasons.' He pointed to his money on the bar.

'Get yourself a soft drink.' Then he said, 'One buck's worth,' to the guy selling the meat raffle tickets who was walking past. The man took his dollar, ripped off a bunch of tickets and handed them over while I ordered a drink.

He laid his tickets out on the bar, sipped his beer and nodded toward the telly.

'Well that was nothing more than the media spinning a hunk of bullshit.'

'You're such a sceptic, Dad.' I'd heard Mum say that many times to him over the years.

'Ahhh, come on. That bunch of poofters don't know nothing more than us, yet they think they can tell us what's going on. You listen closely to what they say next time. There's nothing new in it at all.'

'Yeah, whatever Dad. What's with the overalls?'

'Been helping the police with the line searching.'

'Oh yeah. Where?'

'Paddocks north of the quarry. Bit of surrounding bush.' He didn't mention Denhams Creek, to my great relief, but I had to ask.

'S'pose you're checking the forest tomorrow?'

'Who knows … nothing's been said … be like finding a needle in a haystack if he's lost out there. Hey … what you told me this morning, was that the truth about your face?'

'Yeah, it's what happened.' I felt relieved they hadn't gone searching the forest yet but it was the next obvious place. I hoped we'd done a good enough job.

'Were you drinking? Did you pinch some beers last night too?'

'Nah, just walked into a branch. Like I said. You heading home soon?'

'After the raffle. Few extra draws tonight, never seen the joint so packed.'

'Can I get a lift?'

'Sure. Stick your bike in the ute.'

I smiled for one of the few times that week. Taking a couple of beers to the creek the night before last gave cred to the lie of scraping a tree branch last night. Lies were converging neatly with the truth. I began to think this might actually work out after all, and maybe we were through the worst of it.

In our street, lots of cars were parked out the front of the Debono's. I tried to steer my eyes from that sign when we arrived home at six thirty. Right on dinnertime, which at our house was always straight after the news. Adult lives seemed to revolve around the news. I don't understand why and Nick travelled along okay without it. Nothing can be changed or altered by watching the news, yet it seemed to me like the whole country had a spare half an hour to pry into everybody else's business, before they were able to continue with their own lives. My theory was being cemented. There's nothing they could report that could uncover Debono's body, unless they broke one of us five. And at that stage, that wasn't going to happen because we were convinced they weren't going to bother us again.

In the kitchen, Dad presented Mum with a meat tray and a kiss. He took one look at her dress. 'Where you going all dolled up?'

'I told you there's a church service on tonight. Might be nice for the Debonos if you come along. Replenish your soul too, honey.'

'I'll replenish it down the pub thank you very much. Might get a lift back down with you guys.'

Mum smiled – a difficult smile – given the circumstances. 'Jack, straight after dinner, I want you to get ready.'

'For what?' Disappointment struck me. I knew what she meant.

'The church service. Clean jeans ... and find a nice shirt, please.'

'Why've I gotta go?' It was bad enough having to go on Sundays.

'Jack, I know he wasn't your best friend, but I want you there with me and Tommy, please.'

I replayed her words. "He *wasn't* your best friend." She thought he was dead too.

'Mum, come on, we've said prayers every day at—'

'Jack!' I copped my father's sideways glance.

CHAPTER 20

Days were becoming longer and the sun was setting smack down the middle of Wundowie Street, blinding Mum as she turned the corner to drop Dad off at the pub. We were forced to park on the other side of the primary school, a half a block away from the church. I'd never seen so many cars in Bushmore, or as many people amassed in front of our church. A small portion were Sunday regulars, the rest, just hangers on. Hoping they'd be seen on the news, like Roddy.

They grouped together and spoke in hushed tones within the church grounds. Mum ushered us close to the front doors so we'd get a good seat. Four elderly parishioners manned a roped off area on the grass set aside for the media. I was surprised they actually showed respect and stayed behind the ropes while snapping their photos.

Three carloads of people arrived, Mr. and Mrs. Debono amongst them with other Italians all dressed in black. Women sobbed and wailed, dabbing their eyes with tissues. I didn't recognise any of them and assumed they were relatives. The only colour amongst them was the sky blue dress and white cardigan, worn optimistically by Debono's older sister, Angela. She supported her mother's arm and wiped her tears with a white handkerchief.

Tones lowered in the crowd as Mr. and Mrs. Debono were shepherded past toward the doors. This looked and felt every bit like a Requiem Mass for the Dead. I remember they held one for my Grandfather two days before his funeral. Perhaps that's just the way I saw it because I was the only person here who knew for sure, this was a lead up to a funeral.

My eyes were glued to their sobbing, wretched faces and I realised then I had been sheltered from the realities of death. No one close to me had ever died, except for my Grandparents on Mum's side. They died within two years of each other when I was younger, although both of their deaths were expected because they were sick. Darren Holloway, an older kid from my school who lived in Beaconshire was the only young person I knew of that had died. He drowned in the river last year.

I stood there, like a rock against the pounding ocean of guilt telling myself there was no going back for us. What we'd done was terrible, but it couldn't be undone and no one could be allowed to find out. I couldn't shame my mother in the eyes of the Church. It was unfathomable to do that to her. These people would get over their loss and that body had to stay in the ground, buried forever. I shied away looking for the boys. They sat on their bikes back in the street watching the whole procession. Soupy noticed me, the end of his cigarette glowed as he dragged while grinning away. Not a hint of regret in his heartless soul.

As the Debonos passed I lowered my eyes and after a time, realised I'd been studying every blade of grass surrounding the toes of my shoes, unable to face his family. I think Mum's intention might have been to have a few quiet words of support with Mrs. Debono, but all she did was place firm arms around Tommy and I while goggling at the family like everyone else. I began to head for the door; Mum tugged on my elbow.

'Where are you going?'

'Inside.'

'Wait.'

'No,' I snapped and wished I hadn't.

'Jack, don't be so—'

She paused. '—rude. Disrespectful. What is with you?'

'Just want to go inside, Mum.'

'You'll wait till they enter like everyone else, young man.'

We followed them into the church beneath brand new speakers, set under the porch to broadcast the Mass outside. Father Frost greeted everyone as they passed by, dressed in his white robes and a purple priests' scarf, draped around his neck and hanging down the front of his robe. He tapped me on the shoulder. I froze and shot a glance up to those sick looking, plum coloured cheeks. Tommy ran into the back of me.

Holy eyes cast down on us, yet they were firm. 'Ah, young Jack and Tommy. Can you please pass the collection plate for me tonight?' He had this soft voice. I always thought he'd put it on.

'What?' The last thing I'd expected was for the priest to speak to me.

'The plate. I want you to collect for me, please.' Creepy fingers squeezed a little more on my shoulders. 'Are you okay, Jack?' It was darker in the foyer and I think he noticed the scratches on my face just then because his smile shifted uneasily.

He'd never asked me to hand the plate around before, and Tony Debono was one of his normal plate collectors during Sunday morning services. He was asking me because Debono wasn't here.

Because I'd killed him.

I didn't want to do it. Didn't even want to be here, but I suspected Mum had asked Father Frost if I could play a small part in the Mass tonight, and I couldn't let her down. I gazed into the rear of the church. Parishioners, shoulder to shoulder filled the pews, kneeling and praying. Candles flickered in rows on a golden stand against the chocolate coloured brickwork behind the aisle. I think that's when the full magnitude of what we had done struck me worse than it had all week. For the first time, I realised the tremendous power of guilt and knew I didn't want to enter God's house, but again there was no turning back.

'I can ask someone else?'

I heard the voice again.

'Jack. Jack are you able to—?'

'Yes Father.' I must have phased out a little.

'Okay then, Mr. McQueen and Mr. Upton will collect inside. I'll need you and Tommy to pass two more plates around to the crowd outside.'

'Yes father.' I didn't quite believe it was appropriate for him to be collecting money that night. Perhaps the money was going to the Debono family. Then I questioned why I should even have such an opinion.

Me!

I knew Tommy was happy. He'd missed out on the altar boy gig tonight and had expressed his disappointment at the dinner table, earlier.

Father's fingers slackened on my shoulder. One foot moved in front of the other and I entered, gazing up at the ceiling. It didn't fall in, everything would work out. A camera crew had already set up in the far back corner and in the opposite corner, the half bald man hid behind a large lens aimed toward the altar. We caught up with Mum and once we took our seats, I sensed that uncomfortable holy presence. Up ahead beside the white altar, the green light was lit over the confessional door. Beside it was a red globe, which would click on when someone went inside to confess his or her sins. Could I actually go in there and wrest this guilt from my shoulders. Would Father Frost tell anyone? Was it true he could not disclose any sins heard in the confessional box? Do they really stick to church laws when it comes to murder ... or killing ... whatever it was that we had done?

But the only thing I knew for certain about Father Gray Frost was I couldn't trust him as far as I could kick him. No way was I going into that dark confessional box, plus it didn't matter. If all this hypocritical stuff was true, my road to hell was dead straight.

High-pitched sobbing rose and my eyes shot toward the sound. Mrs. Debono sat wiping tears from beneath a black veil. Black for mourning. How did they know to mourn him? Mr. Debono wore a brave face and placed his comforting hand on his wife's shoulder. They all prayed, except for Debono's sister Angela; her head was bowed but her lips remained still.

She turned and busted me staring at her. I put my head down, quickly. It was almost like she knew what we had done. I saw Debono's face, that dead face, pale and lifeless. I shut my eyes tight, searching for darkness. I found it and tried to sink my mind into the depths of that place until my mum tapped me on the shoulder. Everyone else in the church had stood as Father Frost entered from the front door. The significance of his entry was not lost on me. Normally on Sundays he appeared from the side door beside the altar. Now he paced down the middle aisle, trailed by four altar boys also in white robes. When he reached the Debonos in the front pew, he stopped and murmured something before moving up the altar steps to commence Mass.

Just before the collection and for the third time during Mass, Father Frost asked God for the safe return of Tony Debono. The wailing from his mother and her relatives grew louder and louder. The whole church prayed. Dad's philosophy on God came to mind. He reckons God only exists in the hearts and minds of those who believe in Him, and if they want to believe, that's fine by him. Me, I didn't believe any of it. Still, I prayed for myself and for my mother, just in case God was true and if what we had done ever came out in the full light of day.

I walked toward the altar, trance-like beneath the burning lights and scorching eyes. Tommy followed and we each took a wooden collection plate. I snuck in another glance at the family. Mrs. Debono knelt, weeping and counting rosary beads. Angela cast an eye at me. Our gazes locked once again and her face hardened in an instant. I got the immediate feeling she sought knowledge from me. Knowledge she somehow knew I had. How the hell did she know I knew anything at all? But she knew something; nothing was surer to me.

I dropped my eyes and walked back between the rows, feeling every eyeball on me. It took forever to reach the door and when I did, I felt the cold night air down my lungs. My stomach grabbed, my head lightened, just like last Sunday.

Not again. Please?

Bile rose. The taste of acid sliced my throat like I'd swallowed a razor blade. Don't spew, I told myself. Legs turned to jelly, dizziness overcame me. A hand lifted the plate from my fingers, another hand slipped around my waist. I gasped for more air, steadying myself with one hand on the wall. People moved on the air, switching spots, drifting.

'You all right Jack?' a voice said.

I focused on the still ground, my eyes responded. My vision cleared. I stumbled away from the hand, seeking an open space on my own, all the time swallowing, swallowing. Hungry cameras clicked. I reached the rope. It was only a foot off the ground yet difficult to lift one heavy leg over, let alone two. Fingers gripped my forearm. 'Come on fella,' the calm voice said and I was led over the rope. Finally the hand lowered me softly and my knees hit the grass. Everything stood still and my world returned to a bleak form of normality. I focused on the road. Soupy and boys had left. Thank God.

'Jack ... you okay?' I looked up into the kind eyes of Mr. Wendsley. No matter how cold the weather was, he always wore a neatly pressed short-sleeved shirt, shorts and long white socks stretched over his calves, folded perfectly beneath his knees.

'I'm good ... needed some air.'

He put a caring hand on my back and said, 'Just breathe son, in out ... slowly.'

I did as he told me and my senses returned. My brow cooled, then I saw a grotesque sight. Two fingers. The big finger and the little finger on Mr. Wendsley's right hand were both mangled, bent on weird angles from the top knuckle. They took my mind off my own plight for a bit.

I breathed in and out as he instructed and saw that Tommy had taken charge of both his and my plate, working the crowd on both sides in the fading light. He even hit the media up for money, then walked back inside without me. Mum came out and fussed over me until Mr. Wendsley assured her he'd look after me, then she also went back inside.

After church, mourners crowded around the Debonos like a quarter time huddle at the footy. Mum was right in the mix beneath the floodlights, wanting to offer her love, her support, her thoughts, her prayers. What good would words do for these people? The only words that could help the Debonos had to come from me, and as far as I was concerned those words were locked away forever in a time – almost a week ago – when we killed their damned son.

Mum stood beside the ever-proper Mr. and Mrs. Grimshaw. Their four boys in their Sunday best, hair parted to the left of perfectly manicured heads. Did I *really* used to look like that? Father Frost stood front and centre talking quietly, nodding to people as they touched his hand. I longed to be on my own, so I decided to head around the back of the church to the toilet block where I could rinse my mouth out. I heard yelling and turned to see a cameraman had stepped over the ropes to snap the Debonos from close range. Father placed a hand on the man's shoulder, pointing to the rope.

'Mr. Debono do you have a statement?' A reporter broke the ropes behind him.

'Mr. Debono, your son has been missing for five days … do you believe—?'

An Italian in a black suit and a white, open necked shirt punched the reporter in the forehead. He stumbled back and fell to the ground. Another of the Debonos relatives struck another reporter, who also infringed the ropes. People screamed and spread out. An old lady tripped backwards over the ropes in front of a cameraman. Instead of helping her, the man kept clicking. Two other elderly women rushed to her aid as the first Italian kicked the first reporter in the head while he was on the ground. Mr. Wendsley stepped forward and grabbed the Italian's arm. The man spun and threw a roundhouse hitting Mr. Wendsley in the face, but instead of going down, Mr. Wendsley's jawline seemed to tighten right up, so too did his entire posture. His eyes widened, his left hand cocked in a fist, then all a sudden the Italian's eyes bulged and his body buckled as Mr. Wendsley pulled his right fist from the man's gut. I stood only twenty feet away and had a full view, yet I hadn't seen that punch, thrown faster than lightning. The Italian stumbled back gasping for air. He toppled over the reporter and hit his head on the footpath. Old Mr. Wendsley stood erect; chin high, fists up and rigid, one foot back in a stance. Two more Italians shaped up to him.

'He threw the first punch at me,' he yelled at the men. 'For God's sake I was just trying—'

One of the men lunged at him only to catch a crisp, powerful left fist to the jaw. I heard the smack of bone on bone. The man's head launched backwards and the other man backed off very quickly. Mr. Wendsley's nostrils flared like a racehorse; he eyed the second man up and down until the man stepped away even further. Then he dragged his mate out of Mr. Wendsley's reach. Blood poured from the first man's mouth. I'd known Mr. Wendsley as a non-drinking straight up Catholic – with a slight Irish accent – my entire life. Apparently he grew the finest roses in town, but clearly he had a fighter's past he obviously told no one in Bushmore about. Throughout the scuffle, the media broke the ropes and flew questions and took snap shots of the poor Debonos as they were rushed off to a waiting car. Women cried and men yelled reprisals. Fist fights broke out and the media called out their harrowing questions. All the respect and the restraint shown earlier, was lost in the chaos.

I searched for Mum. She stood on the far side, well back from the ropes beside the Grimshaws, holding Tommy's hand. Car doors slammed shut and the Debonos were whisked away. Bushmore's main copper, Sergeant Regowski and another uniformed officer ran over from the police station and the pandemonium stopped abruptly. People stood around scratching their heads wondering what the hell had happened at our little church, our once quiet little town. Mr. Wendsley and the Italians were supposed to be on the same side, and I'd caused the whole thing.

I wanted to get as far away from that church as I could. I also needed water so I headed toward the primary school where the drinking fountains were located outside the toilet block. Our car was parked on the other side of the school and I could make a quick escape through the playground. As I climbed over the waist high steel fence into the school, a female voice called my name. I quickly turned and was shocked to see Angela Debono hurrying over. Why hadn't she left with the rest of her family? In all the time I'd known her, we might have spoken on no more than a dozen occasions due to our age bracket. Her hair was black, thick and bushy, bouncing toward me. I could see the lines of distress on her face.

She knew I rode motorbikes with her brother and she was going to ask me what my oldies and the police had already asked. I wanted to flee into the school grounds and hide behind a building, or under one of the re-locatable classrooms. Instead, I made the mistake of facing her.

'Jack! Wait ... Jack!'

I shut my eyes and clung to the top of the fence, expecting another dizzy spell.

She reached me, but stayed on the other side.

'I don't know anything.'

'Jack ... what ... what do you mean?'

I looked to the stars and replayed my words. 'I mean ... I ... we don't know anything.'

'What are you talking about Jack. We? Who's we?'

My stomach lurched like a vat was churning deep inside, the taste of spew rose again and I swallowed hard, desperate to keep it down.

'Jack ... what's wrong with you?'

'Nothing.'

'Your forehead ... you're sweating.' She leaned forward; so close I had to force myself to concentrate on the dark hairs above her lips to avoid her eyeballs.

Wind gusted and I felt the cold trickle of sweat and a warm flush on my brow. I wiped my forehead. 'Not feeling too well ... that's all. Might be flu.' Immediately I regretted saying that. She could ask my mum if I had the flu. The lies continued. Lies to protect lies. What kind of person was I? Lying to every individual I came across except for my so-called mates, who had gotten me into this.

She held my gaze, those brown eyes pleaded, they sought. They drilled holes into my mind. I could tell there was so much more she wanted to say, so much more she seemed to know, but how? Then I assured myself she knew nothing.

'Last Sunday, I know he went to the quarry. He told my dad that's where he was going and he rode his motorbike. You saw him there, didn't you Jack?'

Shit.

I'd done such a good job in front of the police and my parents. Now I had to dig my way out of this.

'We ... me, and the other guys haven't seen him.' I shook my head, trying not to look at her, but while my head moved from side to side, my eyes stayed still, fixed on her like they had a mind of their own, trying to betray me. 'We weren't riding in the quarry last week.' Another lie. I'd already told the cops the opposite. Did she know? I had to get away. I took two steps back from the fence, but light-headiness forced me to reach forward and grip the wire rail. I didn't want to chuck up in front of her.

A sharp pain rifled across my stomach then lodged in my right side, like my bowels were full of cement. I'd heard of stones and knew they lodged somewhere in your gut. This felt like a fist sized rock. For the first time all week, I realised I hadn't taken a dump since we'd killed her brother. Perhaps I'd taken one on Monday. I couldn't quite remember.

Mr. Wendsley's voice rang in my head, *"breathe son, breathe."*

'You sure, Jack? I know you ride there every Sunday. Tony told me about your club ... how you were going to let him join.'

'What? No.' He was too old and I had to stop thinking *was*. I wished we'd just let him join. 'He's too ... too old. Tony's run away, hasn't he? It's what ... it's what other kids are saying.'

'No Jack.' Her brow lowered, those eyes bored into me. 'They ... the police, don't think he's run away. I mean they haven't told us as much ... officially ... but I know they don't believe he's just run off. You sure you didn't see him? You must have seen him.'

I scrambled for words 'Yeah ... I mean no ... so ... so what do they think happened ... I mean if he didn't run away?'

'That's what the police are busy finding out. I'd rather not think about—'

I concentrated on my head movement, making sure I nodded up and down. 'Me too.'

'Did he ever talk to you about running away?'

'No ... I mean we weren't friends ... really.'

Aren't friends aren't friends, I hastily reminded myself.

She nodded, giving me a sad look. 'Heard what happened on the bus.' I saw her despair, her hopelessness. Hands hung by her sides. I wanted to help her just as much as I couldn't allow myself to be of any help at all to her.

'It's not a problem, really ... just going to the toilet,' I began to walk off.

'Hey ...' she said. 'He didn't take anything.'

'Jack, wait up.' Another voice. I was relieved to hear Tommy. He ran up behind Angela. 'Where you going?'

'Toilets.'

'Wait for me.'

Tommy was close now. She leaned on the fence, craning her head forward. 'Jack ... no one else knows this ... and you can't tell anyone I told you.' She tightened her lips, shoulders slumped, her face scrunched up like she was fighting back tears. 'They found his bike in the quarry ... today. They found it, Jack. Someone has taken it apart.'

I clamped my eyes dead shut.

'Jack ... Jack?

'I ... I gotta go.' I turned and began to run.

'Jack ... stop. Has something happened?'

'Jack!'

'Jack!'

'Jack ... talk to me ... please?'

I heard her desperate tone. I couldn't run any further. Not from her. She didn't deserve this. I stopped and turned as Tommy scaled the fence. 'I don't know ... how would I know? I don't know anything ... I'm sorry ... I'm so sorry.'

Now I bolted, sprinting toward the toilet block and never heard her voice again. We had killed her only brother and buried his body and only then did I realise how I had grossly misunderstood what we'd done to this family. To Debono. We'd only ever thought of ourselves that fateful afternoon and the consequences for *our* futures. The pain returned in my head like there was a block of wood behind my temple. Could guilt cause pain?

Yes.

This was a type of pain I wished I knew nothing about.

Tommy called after me. This time I didn't stop until my hands found the stainless steel drinking trough. I tried to throw up by coughing and gagging but nothing came out except bile and spit. I thought of sticking my fingers down my throat before I saw a figure in the corner of my eye. Tommy.

*****

That night my dream returned, a more faithful dog than Rex.

They hung me from a tree, your honour.

You are sure of this?

Debono lifted his chin and ran a finger to his scarred neck, snarling at the packed faces behind us. Angela Debono stared back at us, a gruelling determined look.

The judge, dressed in his flowing black gown and white wig, pointed his polished gavel at Roddy. Did you kill him?

NOOO, Roddy screamed. A phonebook as thick as a house brick crashed into the side of his head from behind. Roddy cannoned into Soupy who was chained in the dock beside him. Soupy fell on Cudgy and me. Chains pinged loudly as we found our feet.

DID YOU KILL HIM?

YEEESSSS, Roddy yelled at the judge.

I sentence The Bushmore Liars Club to juvenile prison. No parole. Ever. I stared at the judge's face unable to make out his familiar, elderly features. The gavel came crashing down. The sound echoed through my head.

I woke for the fourth, maybe fifth time that night with a thundering headache and waited with open, terrified eyes for breaking sunlight.

CHAPTER 21

I planned to either wag school or pretend I was sick on the following morning, Friday. But I couldn't stand not knowing the latest news so I dragged my sorry arse out of bed – that sweaty pit where I'd only partially slept once again – and went to school. I couldn't concentrate in class. Kept dozing off for short naps until the teachers woke me. Brother Hobbins even jabbed me in the cheek with a pen during English. After school I went straight home and didn't want to leave the house. I felt safe. No eyes were on me. There was no chance of running into anyone who could interrogate me, or make me feel uncomfortable, make me feel like the lying killer I was.

Dad went to the pub for the third night in a row and stayed there until stumps. Guess he had the same problem and had to hear what was going on. After dinner the phone rang. Roddy and the boys wanted to meet me out the back at the creek. They arrived at dark on their pushies with a dozen cans of beer. Cudgy was missing. Rex went straight to Soupy for a pat. He'd always liked Soupy.

'We're worried about Cudgy,' Meatlips said.

'Why?' My hopes rose, then deflated in one hit. It was way too late for him to squeal now.

'Think he's gonna lag us in to the pigs.'

'You're kidding? Why? Has he said something?'

'Yeah, to me last night,' Roddy said. 'Reckons if we tell a good lawyer what happened, the lawyer could cut a deal for us. You know … go to the cops on our behalf. We would tell the truth … in exchange for no time in juvy. Might get a bond or something. They'd believe it was an accident. They'd have to, right? Be part of the deal and all. Lawyers can do that you know. Cudgy reckons his uncle knows a lawyer who could help us get off.'

'A lawyer, you reckon?' All week I had been thinking about going to the cops or my parents, but hadn't thought about going to a lawyer first. Could that possibly work? 'Cops might believe killing him was an accident, but burying him twice?'

'Exactly what I told him,' Roddy said.

'Won't be long before they start searching the forest.'

'They'll never find him,' Soupy said. 'Guaran' fuckin' teed.'

'What if he says something? You reckon he might have spoken to his uncle already?'

'Dunno ... don't think so,' Roddy said. 'All I know is he's the one most likely to shit himself. Might try and cut his own deal, if we don't agree.'

'What do we do about it?' I asked.

'Had a quiet word to him at school today,' Soupy said. 'Told him if he opens his gob, he'll still go to Juvy and it's worse for dobbers in there. Also told him if they find the body, they can't tell it's us anyway and we'd belt the fucking daylight out of him too. Showed him my little warning.'

'Little warning?'

He reached into his pocket and pulled out something long and silver. I heard a crisp flick. A blade appeared.

'Jees, Soupy ... what the hell?' He still had his other arm over Rex, patting him. I wanted to call my dog over, but didn't through genuine fear that something else might be going down here and I didn't want to show my hand. I knew he wouldn't hurt my dog, but I was still scared.

'Don't worry about Cudgy. We're not gonna stick him. Might do his mum's dog though, you know, just a little warning not to say anything.'

Soupy had this evil side to his grin. I saw my dog's trusting eyes and clicked my tongue. His ears pricked and he came over and sat with me. I breathed a sigh of relief and wrapped my fingers inside his collar.

Did Cudgy somehow know the cops had found the bike? These guys obviously didn't know, or they would have told me.

'Saw Cudgy down the pinnies earlier,' Soupy said, lighting a smoke. 'Guess he wouldn't have shown up if he'd said something yet. Might go over to his joint in the morning and suss him out again. You coming?'

'Nah. Working with the old man.' I lied, knowing Dad would have the mother of all hangovers in the morning and wouldn't get up for work.

I'd already decided I was getting out of this craziness and planned to head out to see Old Nick. Might just be what I needed to calm my nerves after such a horrible week.

'What you doing for the rest of the weekend?' Soupy asked.

'Mum wants me to hang about with Tommy.' Truth was, I didn't want to be near these guys at all on the weekend. Last night's run-in with Debono's sister had shaken me up.

Soupy now had this cunning look about him and focused it on me. Then as if he picked up on the fact I didn't trust him, he passed over his smoke.

I didn't want to, but still took a few drags. For some reason beer weakened my resistance and I didn't feel the dizziness I normally felt. I was on my second can and the beer wasn't having its usual effect on me either, and I began to think Soupy had just threatened me, and my dog. So I told them about the cops finding Debono's bike.

'Fuck me, Gillo! How'd you find that out?' Meatlips asked. Now he was the one who wore an accusing look.

I didn't want to tell him I'd spoken to Debono's sister so I said, 'My old lady heard it.'

'How the hell would that bitch find out?' Roddy said.

I don't know why I didn't thump him, and still wish I had because it was my last opportunity, ever. But I held my nerve.

'How the fuck do I know … probably heard it down the church.'

Soupy took a last drag and butted his smoke out. 'Heard there was a dust up down there last night.'

'That was crazy shit,' I said and told them all about it, happy to get off the subject of the bike.

We finished the beers off and I was quite glad when the guys left because they were our last words, face to face.

CHAPTER 22

Saturday, I woke with a splitting headache and a furry taste in my mouth, then remembered the beers and the drags of Soupy's cigarettes and vowed never to smoke again. I showered and brushed my teeth twice before breakfast then told Mum I was meeting the guys over at Cudgy's house.

'Honey, please, your father and I want ... we think you should stay home until we're sure it's safe to be able to go and hang around with your friends like you used to.'

'No way Mum, you let me out, on Thursday.' I dropped my head, unable to believe it. She'd changed her mind again. A complete backflip and she wanted me cooped up for a whole weekend. A prisoner of my own stupidity.

Dad's voice trampled through my head. *"Do as your mother says."* He hadn't appeared from the bedroom yet and may not for a while. I had to get out before he woke up.

I decided not to argue. Instead, I went to my room, scribbled another note and left it on my dresser.

STOP WORRYING ABOUT ME. YOU CAN'T KEEP ME
HERE LIKE THIS.
XXX JACK.

And as soon as I figured Mum was going about her normal routine in the main part of the house, I escaped out the back door. Rex followed. I couldn't afford to get busted going out the driveway, so I left on my new racer through the back gate and down along the creek.

I stashed my bike in some bushes and headed over the valleys until I was looking down from the ridge towards Nick's shack.

No smoke.

My first instinct was to flee, the setting wasn't right. Instead, I circled the ridge until I could see the west side of his camp. His fishing rods were on the roof so he wasn't at the river. Perhaps he was hunting. Something deep inside told me he wasn't. Rex and I started walking down the slope, keeping behind the trees as much as I could. A low warning rumble came from deep within Rex as we moved around the edge of the camp. I patted him, in an effort to appease him as I approached the flap and called out for Nick. No answer came.

My mind yelled at me to go home, but as I had done so often in the past week, I ignored common sense and gently pulled the flap across a smidgen and poked my head in. All was deadly quiet, until a strong hand grabbed my wrist and wrenched me in. Rex barked and muscled his way in between my legs. I saw the pistol in the shoulder holster outside a white shirt, a hand on the butt, ready. Rex snarled, baring his teeth.

'Jack Gillings!' Detective Bottomly said, glaring down at Rex. 'Quieten your mutt up, boy.'

He had a chiselled jaw like a newsreader. I struggled with the rapid-fire speed of his speech and his thick, Scottish accent. It sounded like *"quitnyamuddup"*. Under tremendous confusion, I finally worked it out and said, 'Let go of my wrist and he'll be fine.'

He released his grip. I rolled my wrist to get the blood circulating and stroked my dog. His body shuddered.

'What a turn up? How come you're here, young Jackie?'

Jackie?

He said it with a "u" like "Juckie". I became nervous and tense. No one except my mum had ever called me Jackie.

How come *you're* here? I wanted to ask, studying his face. It was hard lined with deep crevices between his nose and cheeks. They disappeared under his moustache, trimmed square like a yard broom. The wry smile scared me along with those beady eyes I recognised from our last meeting at my house. I questioned why a cop was here and a hot flush swept over me as the obvious dawned. They were blaming Nick. A boy goes missing. A vagrant lives in the forest, who no one except for me knows anything about. How could I not have thought of this scenario earlier?

I looked him up and down, speechless, then my eyes settled on the gun. He moved his hand away. Rex snapped out another bark as the flap opened and in walked the taller detective, Hayden. He gazed down at me, hands on hips and sighed.

'Aye. You haven't answered my question, young Jackie,' Bottomly said.

I wondered if they followed me, but surely I would have noticed so I figured they'd been waiting here.

I stayed quiet, remembering what I'd heard on the telly. *"Anything I said would be used against me"*. I knew that much about a person's rights as to remain silent.

'Do you know this man they call Old Nick?'

I had to decipher his sentence before my trembling mouth deserted me. 'I … I've been here—' I should've shut up.

'Tell us, luddy.'

'I … I met him once before.'

'No, luddy.' Bottomly shook his head very firmly and very slowly. His eyes locked on mine. 'No. You've been here more often than that.'

I waited for him to elaborate, but he didn't. He stayed silent. He knew that I knew he was right. I was under interrogation and he was waiting for me to dob myself in. For what? I didn't know. The expression *give a person enough rope and he'll hang himself* leapt to my mind. My science teacher, Mr. Kronberg used it a lot to catch out kids who he thought were lying. Bottomly gave me a little rope and I told my first lie to him. He was all over me like a rash.

'He's your friend, isn't he?'

I swallowed, lost for words.

'Aye Jackie, tell me the truth now.'

'Y … yes.' I tried to think of what Meatlips might say in the same position. None of his words came to mind, like there was a blank space in my head.

'Jackie.' He held out his palm toward the tree stump Nick used as a seat. 'Sit down, please.'

My legs moved slowly toward the stump. One wrong step and I worried that I'd trip over it. I sat down and faced the detectives. Things only got worse for me, as now they were able to stare down from a greater height.

'Jack, can you tell us anything about this man? We need to know everything we can about him.'

'Why?'

'Jack, a boy has gone missing.' He deliberately slowed his speech so he wouldn't mince his words. 'The man who lives here has also disappeared. Another boy turns up at his hut. I'm a detective. In my world two and two make a crime.'

All I could do was stare at his lips in an attempt to avoid the interrogating eyes.

'Jack. Has this man ever said anything inappropriate or done anything—?'

'No.' And then I worked out where he was heading. 'NO! NO! Definitely not! NO! Nick is my friend, he's a good person. He doesn't have anything to do with—'

I realised I had gone too far. He twisted his head and intensified his gaze. 'What Jack? What doesn't he have anything to do with?'

I held my tongue, knowing I had to answer. 'He's … he's run away.'

Bottomly placed a foot on the stump right beside me, resting his hands on his knee so close I felt a draft of air release through his nose as he sighed. 'Aye, Jack. Between you and me I can tell you that boy has not run away. It's important you answer my question honestly. Do you know where this man might be?'

I scanned around the shack. None of Old Nick's cookware and other worldly possessions appeared to be missing. I realised somehow Nick would be smart enough to know the cops were here.

'No,' I said, 'wouldn't have a clue. How would I know? Came looking for him, same as you.'

'Aye Jack, but you do know him well enough to come down here.'

I nodded.

'Do your parents know you're down here? Do they know you come here at all?'

I envisioned the flash of disgust on my mum's face. As sure as hell she'd find out now.

I stared at the floor. 'No.'

'All right, Jackie. You're to come with me.'

He led me by the arm back out through the flap, then turned to address Hayden. 'Be on your toes. I'll be back, soon as I can.'

I felt Nick's eyes on us as he led me through the bush and back to the dirt road where he'd left his car. We picked up my bike along the way and he took Rex and me home, where my mum was waiting at the door. She sent me to my room and spoke with the officer in the lounge room before he drove off in his car.

My bedroom door opened. I was lying down facing the window.

'Honey—?' She sat on the bed and stroked my forehead.

'Honey, what were you doing out in the forest visiting that man?' I could hear the waver, the fear in her voice, see the trembling of her lips and I wanted to assure her Nick wasn't the man they all thought he was.

I stared up into her innocent, trusting eyes. What was she thinking of me now?

I could make it end just by telling her, just by opening my mouth and saying words, speaking the truth. Had I done so, I would have avoided the horrendous events of the following day, but of course I didn't.

'He's a friend, Mum. That's all. We go surfing and fishing together. He's teaching me heaps of things.' I fought off tears. 'He didn't do what they think he did. I promise.' I was part angry at her, part angry at the police and even more angry at myself because I knew the right decision was to tell her and the police everything, yet I was unable to make the right decision on my own. I was piss weak.

'He's wanted by the police, honey. No one knows who he is and surely you understand why we can't let you go there anymore. You do understand, don't you Jack?'

I nodded, despite knowing that even though I was just nodding, I was simply lying again. Everyone I spoke to I lied to.

The first chance I got I'd have to leave here and find Old Nick, in case he didn't know they were after him. I felt certain he knew anyway, felt sure that he saw me there today. But what if he didn't? He'd be arrested and go to jail for the outstanding assault charges alone, and now they wanted to question him for a murder he knew nothing of. 'He didn't do it, Mum.'

'Jack, honey … listen to me. The police have found certain things in the quarry and they know the man in the bush has been seen there recently.'

'What?' I said, shocked. 'I've never seen him there, Mum. That's crazy.'

'It's not crazy, Jack. He's been hanging around there. You must understand why you can't go into the bush or out to the quarry.'

I listened in total disbelief. Who would have seen him at the quarry? No one. Nick had never even mentioned the quarry once to me.

Who?

I cast my mind back to the previous night. Meatlips had been extraordinarily quiet. Roddy and Soupy would never talk to the cops, but Meatlips would. He'd have the guts to ring them. It was the only way the cops could find out because no one else we knew went into the quarry. I didn't understand why they didn't tell me about it last night. Why didn't they bring me in on the story? I had to speak to Meatlips first. I had to get rid of Mum.

'Sure, Mum,' I said. 'I understand.'

'Please don't leave the house again. This is very very important to your father and I.'

'Okay, okay. I just want to be on my own, Mum.'

She took a second, then wiped my forehead in her loving mum way and left me to lie there, staring at the ceiling. I heard the laundry door shut. She'd gone outside so I went to the lounge room and grabbed the handset, took it back to my room and rang Meatlips. His dad told me he wasn't home. I tried Roddy's. They weren't there either so I rang the pinball shop. Joe, the owner answered and called to Meatlips. Seconds later I heard his voice.

'Hey Gillo, come down, we're out the front.'

'I can't. The old lady won't let me out and I'm already in trouble for pissing off once.'

'Warden's on duty, huh.'

All of a sudden I hated him too. He'd always prodded me about my mum being strict. It never worried me before and he normally wasn't mean about it, unlike Roddy.

'You told the cops you'd seen Old Nick at the quarry. Why?'

'Jack, come on mate. What are you on about?'

Jack. He called me Jack. I couldn't remember the last time he called me by my first name. I could tell by the sinister tone of his voice, he was behind this.

Meatlips, the only one with nothing to lose. As I held the phone, I closed my eyes and recalled my dream that had haunted me all week. Even though he was on the other end of the line, I saw his face as a truckload of dream-induced déjà vu rolled through my head. I saw that judge's face. He was older, the birthmark had all but disappeared beneath that white wig in my dream. Meatlips, the puppeteer, manipulating, controlling this whole situation without being a part of any of it, even in my sleep. Playing games with our lives at arm's length. I hadn't seen it, but my subconscious did somehow. Now he was toying with the life of an innocent man. I wanted to see his face. I wanted to rip his head clean off his shoulders.

'Get around here, you scumbag.'

'Ease up, Gillo. Round where?'

'My joint. You might be able to treat the others like idiots, that's because they are. Not me. I want to see you right now, arsehole. Meet you at the back fence.'

There was a pause. 'No, Jack. I'm not coming around.'

'Just like I thought. You dobbed Old Nick into the cops.'

There was another long pause over the line before he spoke. 'You think the cops wouldn't put it all together, eventually. You think other people in the town wouldn't have told them a deadbeat hobo is living in the forest nearby.'

'You just made sure of it, huh. You lying dirty arse.'

'Did it for you, mate.'

I slammed the phone down so hard, the casing cracked.

*****

Dad came home a short time later and within minutes, I heard him trampling down toward my room. The door burst open, then he slung it shut so hard my Joan Jett poster fluttered and nearly fell off the wall. He tore shreds off me for breaking the phone and stressing out Mum. In no uncertain terms he warned me about Nick, warned me about going back into the forest or the quarry. He warned me about what a prick I was becoming and if I left the house again without telling either of them, the strap was coming out no matter how old I was. He also warned me I would not get my apprenticeship with him, either.

'You'll go to that school for as long as I send you there you little shit,' was his last comment before he stormed out and flung the door shut so hard I thought it might bounce off its hinges.

CHAPTER 23

Sunday, I threw what might even be described as a tantrum. Dad had left for work early, telling Mum he had a lot of catching up to do and didn't ask if I wanted to go and help. After he blew the crap out of me yesterday, Mum must have spoken to him and reminded him of the circumstances of the week, because he came back into my room half an hour later and apologised. He never would have done that on his own and I think he was still angry with me. But there was another reason why he hadn't asked me to come to work. Despite the pub not being allowed to open on Sundays, I knew that after eleven o'clock the publican would open the back door for the regulars. Dad would be in there like a rat up a drainpipe, catching up on the man gossip as Mum called it. This week there'd been plenty. He'd taken me through the back door before on Sundays, but I got the feeling he was happy to leave me in Mum's hands this time.

After another soul-searching night of anger, sketchy dreams and jagged, broken passages of time I put down as sleep, I went to the toilet and tried. Nothing happened again, couldn't even cut a fart so I stayed in my room all morning listening to East, my favourite Cold Chisel tape. I wanted to get out but where could I go? Dad had been so angry the day before and I didn't dare cross him again. After what Meatlips had told the police about Old Nick, I didn't want to see any of the guys either. I was sure he'd worded them all up, even Cudgy, and I was also sure they were bullshitting me about Cudgy apparently wanting to lag us all in to a lawyer.

They were testing *me* out, not Cudgy and I fell for it. They thought I was the weak link and the bastards were right.

I couldn't even go down to the pinnies because they didn't open until twelve on Sundays. But despite my fear of crossing Dad, I knew I had to get out. There was only one place I could go. One place I had to go.

Mum knocked on my door at ten. I knew what she wanted.

'Jack honey, hurry up and get ready for Mass.'

'Not going.'

'You get ready, NOW, young man.'

'I'm crook.' As far as I was concerned I never wanted to step foot in that place again.

'Don't you lie to me!'

'Not going, Mum.'

That's when I started going off. We argued and yelled like that for several minutes but in the end – despite the fact this was new ground for me to tell her I'm not going to church – I knew I'd win because the self-inflicted peer group pressure Mum put on herself by not attending church, would be too great. Especially after this week.

Minutes later she came back to my room and this time she didn't knock, just flung the door open.

'If you move from this house, so help me God, you'll be grounded for a year.'

The second I heard the Kingswood back out the drive, I ran outside to find the smart bitch had chained and padlocked both my bikes together.

I had to find Old Nick. I knew he'd be hiding at the house and the quickest way out there was by motorbike. So I locked Rex in my room and ran nearly all the way to Roddy's, but couldn't risk confronting either him, or the others. I had my own decisions to make and Old Nick would help me work this out. I knew I had to tell the cops and my parents, I wanted this to be over.

Roddy lived on the northeast edge of town on the other side of the Emerald River, so I stopped at the Wundowie Street Bridge and waited patiently. My mind was busy stewing over my poisoned thoughts. Roddy was never home after lunch on Sundays. Since the quarry was closed, I knew he'd go down to the pinnies. Soon, my reward came. Just after lunch, the four of them rode over the bridge above me heading into town. I walked back up the bitumen road to Roddy's, wondering if my bike was still in one piece, concerned they might have even torched it. I knocked on the back door, his mother answered.

'Think he's gone out with the others.'

'Thanks,' I said. 'Might grab my bike from the shed.'

'Go for it, luv.' Puffs of smoke escaped from her gaping mouth and nostrils as she waved me off.

I went to the shed and my nerves made me knock, just in case. I'd never knocked before even though the boys were gone. I'd never even asked Roddy's mum if I could go to the shed. Normally we'd by-pass the house and go straight in, but this was different, unfamiliar territory. I wasn't welcome here anymore.

I nudged the door in. My bike stood in the far corner, thankfully all in one piece. I filled it with juice (we'd all chipped in for) and took off for freedom. Free from my oldies and most importantly, free from my former best mates, forever. My motorbike was the last tie to them.

I raced across the back of town, leaving a trail of orange dust rising off the gravel roads and headed down the Coast Road, out past the Dartmoore Road turnoff leading to the quarry, cordoned off by police tape. I kept to the dirt roads, riding around the edge of the forest. I passed a police car parked in the front of a driveway; officers were talking to the owner. They didn't bother to chase me, an unlicensed kid on an unregistered bike.

Soon after I came across another cop parked up at a farmhouse. Something was going on in the area, I didn't know what, but minutes later when I was close to the turnoff for the Turnbull Track, a police siren wailed behind me. I couldn't get caught again so I headed straight into the forest, found a bush track and didn't look behind.

I navigated my way through the trees and came out further along the Turnbull Track. I left my bike out of sight near the stump, listening for the rumbling of a cop car over the corrugations behind me, but thankfully none appeared. I knew they weren't far away, searching every property in the area. I had to find Nick first so I ran up around the bend. Finally I reached the house. The property looked deserted as always. The door, locked. I wandered around the perimeter, calling softly for Nick, peering through lifeless windows. The blinds were half up. I could see part way into each room. No sign of anyone.

I knew where he hid the key but didn't want to go inside. The cops still had five or six properties to look through before they reached this area. I was ahead of them and decided to check the shed. When I opened one side of the barn door, daylight spilled in to reveal the ute in its place, parked on the dirt floor. I half expected Nick to run out, but as I'd already called his name several times, I guessed he wasn't here after all. The surfboards were untouched, wetsuits hung about, dry. None of the rods had been moved. Everything seemed in its place. A hand touched my shoulder. I nearly leapt through the roof.

'Jack, what are doing here?' He wore a Driza-Bone full-length jacket and his brown, wide brimmed bushman's hat, blending him into the surrounding scrub. The jacket was covered in dirt, like he'd been sleeping on the ground.

'Nick, the cops are on their way, you have to leave. Now.'

'They came to my hut yesterday. Saw them first, luckily.'

'I know. I was there in the afternoon. They caught me and took me home.'

'Saw that too. Did you say anything about me … about the house?'

'No way.'

'Good. Don't know why'd they're bothering me after all these years ... hey.' His brows firmed. 'How the hell did you know they were after me?'

I stared at him in disbelief. Of course! I was his only contact with the outside world and he didn't know about Debono's disappearance. How could he?'

'Nick ... that's not the reason. I got a lot to tell you. Something's happened in Bushmore ... last weekend. Let's get out of here, I can explain it once we're clear of the house.'

'Follow me.'

He led me through the bush over a rise and we trekked across two more valleys. Stabbing cramps returned in the left side of my gut. I did my best to ignore them and pressed on until we rested where a creek pooled and fed a small waterfall a couple of feet high.

'We're safe here,' he said and we sat down on some rocks. He studied me. 'Your face ... you okay?'

'Scratched it.'

'I can see that, but you look thin. You stressed about something?'

I didn't know where to start. I wasn't ready, unsure of how far I could go with Nick, so I didn't answer.

'How did you know the cops were looking for me?'

I couldn't get the truth out. I thought about only telling him enough to get him to leave here and move elsewhere.

I bit my lip.

'Jack, you know you can talk to me about anything.'

I nodded, swallowing hard.

Here goes.

'A boy from our town has disappeared, last Sunday. They think you did it.'

'Did what ... what the hell are you talking about?'

'You gotta get out of here. Cops think you've got something to do with this kid disappearing.'

'That explains the helicopters.' He gave a worried look, his eyes rolled up toward the sky. 'Saw 'em through the week over the forest.'

'Yeah, searching the quarry too.'

'Cops aren't my only concern.' His eyes scanned the bush. I'd seen him look about with caution several times on the way here.

'What do you mean?'

'Saw trackers in the bush this morning.'

'Trackers?'

'Yeah, three men, tracking me, all with rifles near my camp. Managed to lead them deep into the bush where I was able to lose them, then sort of put it together. First the cops came, then I saw these clowns studying my foot prints. Thought I might be safe here, but if the cops are coming along the road? Hell! You say a kid's missing. How old?

'Sixteen.'

'Shit.' He rubbed his chin. 'Pretty good excuse for vigilantes, don't you think?'

'Vigilantes?'

'Hunting parties. If they suspect I've done something terrible to a kid, they'll also think they've got a right to protect the town and all that bulldust. There might be more than one group of hunters out. Some of these country hacks just need an excuse to go out and shoot someone.'

I knew exactly what he meant. Most of them drank with my dad in the pub.

'How do you know the cops are coming to the house?'

'Saw them searching properties back up the road.'

'Yeah ... once that's over, it'll be fine.' His nervous eyes glanced around the forest. I had no idea what he was going through, being hunted for a crime he didn't commit. But I knew what I must do.

I held my face in my hands, sucked up air and spoke more into my palms than I did to Nick when I said, 'We did it, Nick.'

'Did what?'

'We killed him ... accidentally.'

I stared into the darkness of my hands. My eyelids became heavy and I felt like I could sleep for a year. I had done what I'd longed to do all week. I had told someone.

'Jack ... killed who? What the hell have you gotten yourself into, young fella?'

Over the next half an hour I sat there and told him everything about our club, our stupid rules, the fight on the bus. Last Sunday at the quarry and the events of the past week. Everything. All except the bit that his neck cracked when I first kicked him. I couldn't tell anyone that.

'My God, Jack. If this is all true, and I have no reason to doubt you, then you have to tell the police ... and your parents. The parents of that poor boy.'

'I know ... I know, Nick. Just don't know how to do it. They're good people and I want to do the right thing, but I don't want to go to jail, juvenile detention or wherever they'll send me. What if I'm sixteen when my trial comes around? Will they send me straight to prison?'

'Listen, if you go to the police and tell the truth there's a good chance you won't be sent to Juvenile Detention. They'll believe you when you tell them where the body is.'

'It would mean dobbing on my mates. I'll be sending them to juvy.'

His eyes narrowed. 'You can't go near them. You must realise if you go to them, you might not be able to convince them this is the right thing. I've come to know you Jack ... you're better than this. Do you believe in yourself?'

'Yes.'

'Then you have to do this on your own, son. You have to be honest with yourself. Stand up like a man.'

There they were. The words I'd been waiting for all week. Stand up like a man. I'd seen those words, just hadn't heard them. I'd seen Mr. Wendsley stand up for himself when he was challenged. I lifted my chin like I'd seen Mr. Wendsley do. I wanted to be proud again. Like I used to be.

Stand up like a man.

My father would have said the same thing, had I possessed the balls to own up to him. Tears flowed. Tears of great affection for my dad. It's exactly what he would have said and I didn't give him half the chance. Then I wiped away those tears and fought back more, sniffing hard. They weren't getting out. Fuck this, I thought. Stand up like a man. Those were the words I'd wanted, needed to hear all week and I should have gone to my dad. He would've protected me.

I turned it over and over in my mind and for the first time I no longer felt scared of the others. I didn't care what they would do. I had to stand up to them too. I knew there was no way I'd be able to convince them to change their minds. At that point I realised I hated Meatlips and Roddy. Soupy, I held a minor ounce of respect for, although now that I look back, I don't know why, perhaps it was his racing ability. Cudgy was just a gutless lamb. He'd only tell the truth if the others told him to. So that ruled them all out. 'They won't do it.'

'Are you scared of them, Jack? Have they threatened you?'

I thought of Soupy holding my dog, the knife in his other hand. 'No.' I felt a firm resolve building up in me.

'Then you have to leave here and go straight home and tell both your parents. If one's not there, then make a call and get them both home, because they have to be told at the same time. I can't speak for them, but I can tell by who you are that you're a product of good people and they'll look after you, Jack. They love you and they'll make sure you got a lawyer and all that, and they'll take you to the police.

'You hear me, Jack … Jack?' I heard his fingers snap.

'Yeah ... sure. I'll do it.' This was the right thing to do all along and I hadn't been able to work it out for myself. At fifteen ... I still had to be told. It was the crayfish thing all over again. How was I ever going to work the rest of my life out?

'I'm glad I came to you, Nick.'

'That's what friends are for. We're mates Jack, no matter what? We can't take back our actions. They're in the past, but we can own them, be honest and deal with them and that's how you will measure yourself as a man in the future. You've made a horrible ... horrible mistake. We all make mistakes, but we're mates and that's the reason you came to me.' His long arm slipped over my shoulder and pulled me in tight. 'I know you're a good kid and you can begin to fix this.

'You didn't mean it, so it's not murder. Just a horrible accident and as for your part, you did the wrong thing by hiding the body. The only way forward is with the truth. You have to release your conscience and once you do, it'll be the first step. You owe that much to this boy's family, they need to know everything. But you can't tell any more lies.'

I nodded. For the first time all week I understood everything. 'What about you, Nick?' Why don't you go and fix up your wrong? Get out of here and go back to Queensland, live a normal life with your family and friends.'

'Wish it was that simple, mate. You see, what I did wrong was of the consequence of the wrong done to me. The Government don't recognise it was wrong to send men off to a war in Asia and that's why I got into the trouble I did.'

'So you believe what you did was right?'

'No mate. I *know* what I did was right and this is what I want you to learn. There is a world of difference between a belief and a knowledge. A belief is in the mind, knowledge is fact. You know it, you don't only just believe it anymore.'

I thought about God.

'I know my stance against the war was right and as a consequence of that, I assaulted those two officers. Just like you have a knowledge right now that you have to fix this. I make sacrifices for what I did and living in the forest is one of those sacrifices, but I will never go to jail for it. I *know* what's right and what's wrong.'

'Do you believe in God?'

'What's God got to do with your predicament—?'

'Just tell me.'

He shook his head a touch. 'Now, I wasn't going to bring that up because I was also brought up in the church and I don't want to influence your faith—'

'Don't bullshit me with that crap, Nick. I don't believe half of it anyway. If I want someone to pussyfoot around religion, then I'll go to my mum ... or my dad for that matter because they both sit on opposite sides of the fence. Christ, my dad reckons people used to think heaven was up in the clouds, in the stars, but we've been there now so they tell us heaven's in another dimension. My dad says they moved the goalposts to make it work. Tell me what you really think.'

Now he was busily nodding. 'Do I believe? Well I've had a lot of spare time to think over the years and I guess I do believe in God. I talk to him a lot. Just don't believe in religions. The forest allows me to be away from all that stuff.'

'Huh?' Now I was really confused. 'How can you believe in God and not religion?'

'Well, religion is nothing but the perfect business model manufactured by men in power to get their hands on money. Control people's thinking and you control their money. It's simple. No one can prove there's a God, that's why they call it faith. Religions trade on their own theories, *"we're right ... we're the chosen ones ... fire and brimstone for non-believers"* and all that rubbish. What their real message is, is the one they're not saying, which is *"you're not on the right team, you're not the chosen one, but if you sign up with us, you will be."* There are so many religions, only difference is in the fine print. Fact is, they can't all be right so they trade on their different rhetoric and beliefs. But in the wash, they're all selling the same thing, the ultimate life after death insurance policy. We're programmed from the earliest years to believe we need God. Yet God needs you, otherwise they can't trade, can they? Everyone needs money, how else can they operate in society?'

'Suppose so,' I said. 'Unless your name's Nick.'

'Unless your name's Nick,' he repeated. Despite our predicament, we both found a grin.

'Guess I never thought of it that way. Often there's hundreds of dollars in the church plate as it's passed around, and there's the envelopes some people use so others can't see how much they give.'

'Watering the money tree, Jack. I like to believe in the big fella, but we've gotta look after ourselves down here, too. If I went to war, God wasn't going to help me dodge those bullets and He didn't help me escape from Queensland. Now the same people in different uniforms want to question me for murder. God won't help me there either.' His large comforting hand of friendship firmed on my shoulder. 'You're the only one that can do that now.'

'I'll make it right Nick, I promise. Soon as I get back.'

'Good man.'

'You'd like my dad.'

'I think I would. Does he play chess?'

'Nope.'

'Might get a chance to teach him one day. Wish we could sit down and have a game ourselves before you go see the police, but we must move on. You ready to do this?'

I nodded. I was a hundred per cent ready to fix this, no matter what.

'How'd you get here?'

'Motorbike. It's back at the stump.'

'Come on, I'll take you there.'

'What about the cops up on the road.'

'What about em,' he said grinning. 'They'll never—' Then before he could finish speaking, he raised a hand up in a stop-like gesture to keep me still.

'Get down,' he said pushing me onto the wet ground beside the rocks. 'Stay there. Don't move.'

'Why?' But he disappeared into the bush.

I waited. The forest became deadly quiet. No birds chatted or sang. No wind blew. Voices came. Quiet, yet the unmistakable voices of men were coming my way.

I poked my head up from behind the rock and saw three men. They passed close by, three of the four Botwin brothers from town; all dressed in camouflage gear and aiming their rifles toward the area Nick had ran into. Bruce and Frankie told Loopy Lenny to stay where he was. They walked forward, hunched down. Minutes later I heard a shot followed by a man yelling in agony in the forest.

'NICK!' I screamed.

Lenny raised his rifle to his shoulder, ready to shoot.

'NO!' I ran toward him, he spun, the rifle levelled. 'Don't shoot!' I swear before the blast rang out I saw black eyeballs spinning inside those crazy white, widened eyes. My legs went from under me. My world went blank.

CHAPTER 24

I drifted in and out, listening to fragments of conversations in the place where I was held.

'Do you think he's telling the truth?' It sounded like my mum.

'Who knows till he wakes up.' Definitely my dad's voice.

Time and space sort of happened. More voices came and went.

'It passed right through flesh and muscle mainly. Took out a piece of the underside of his collarbone. He's very lucky. We expect him to make a full recovery.'

I had no idea who said that before drifting back to the comfortable abyss, not knowing how much time passed before I heard, 'They've asked if they can see him.'

My former mates?

'No ... No ... Noooo.'

Mum's voice said, 'I think he just whispered no. He knows what we're saying.'

I fell back to that peaceful nothing.

Then came more voices, the heavy accent. 'Aye. We have to rely on Jack once he wakes up.' A door clicked shut.

Sometime after, I slipped easily into the real world and saw my mum's eyes, all blurry and tearful.

'Jack ... darling.' She held my hand.

I opened my mouth and tried to ask what happened and where I was. No words came out.

'Don't try and speak.'

I recalled the blast and tried to move my left shoulder. Nothing happened as if it wasn't there.

'Honey, don't move.'

'What's … what's going on?'

She wiped my brow. 'You've been shot, honey. It was a terrible accident.'

Memories flooded back, the blood, the burning. I'm in the backseat of a police car, an officer nursing me. The smell. My bowels had loosened. How nice and comfortable it felt to have moist shit running down my legs.

A nurse came in. 'Good morning you brave young man. Nice to see you're awake.' She checked my pulse and the drip attached to my right arm. 'You're one lucky boy—'

'Mum … what happened to Nick?'

'We don't really know, sweety.'

'Was he hurt?'

But I was interrupted by the nurse who said to my mum, 'They want to come in.'

She gave a horrified look. 'Good God, can't they wait?'

'They wanted to be informed straight away,' the nurse said, before leaving.

'Honey,' Mum said. 'Do you remember anything?' There was an urgency to her voice. 'Do you remember what you said to the police?'

The door opened and in walked Bottomly, followed by the Detective Hayden.

'Morning, Jack.' He turned to my mum. 'How is the lud?'

'Awake,' she said, pressing her lips together. She flicked me a glance, her mouth hung in the corners. I saw fear in her eyes, worry on her face.

My main concern was Nick. 'What's going on?' I asked as a tall, silver-haired man in a white coat entered. A doctor, I assumed. 'You have to leave,' he informed the two officers and held the door open, then followed them outside. I didn't see the police for the rest of my first conscious day.

The doctor returned and asked a bunch of questions and filled in a chart, which hung on the back of my bed. 'You're going to be fine Jack,' he said. 'Surgery was a success and you'll be bouncing round the footy field in no time.'

He left us in the room. Dad arrived soon after. Mum seemed on tenterhooks, asking me how I felt and wiping my cheeks, but there was stuff she wasn't saying to me through her loving caresses. I knew she knew the truth, everyone did, although I didn't know how. She left for coffee. Dad and I were alone.

'How do they know?' I asked.

He rubbed his forehead, sighed and then said, 'Listen Jack, on the way to the hospital you told the police some wild story—'

Memories returned in patches. The Botwins carrying me up the slope, the police coming down into the forest.

'Nick ... what's happened to him? Where is he?'

He shook his head.

I stared at him in horror. 'Wh ... what?' I waited for Dad to tell me the worst news. Nick was dead.

'He got away, but not after he put a bolt from a crossbow in Bruce Botwin's knee.'

Relief flooded through me as more memory trickled in. I remembered the agonising scream. The crack of the rifle before I was shot.

'They fired on Nick first. I know they did. They were hunting him down, Dad.'

'That may be. The police will sort it out. Bruce is all right, ripped the bolt out himself, but that bastard Lenny's where he belongs. In jail.'

I recalled his eyes and knew that psycho nutcase just wanted to shoot something, anything ... me. I remembered lying on the back seat of the police car telling an officer – who had my blood all over him – what had happened to Tony Debono. Up until now I thought I'd dreamt it.

'What the hell were you doing down there, Jack?' Dad asked.

'I had to warn Nick.'

'It wasn't any of your business, mate.'

'Yes it was. I caused it all. It's all true.'

'What's true?'

'What I told them … it's all true.'

'Son, you were in shock. I've spoken to a lawyer in town. He said—'

'Don't care, Dad. I did it. I told them the truth.'

He nodded slowly, contemplating. 'We'll work our way through this, then.'

'Am I going to prison?'

'They haven't told us if there are to be any charges laid yet.'

The cops took my statement the next day – Wednesday. Dad was present, Mum waited outside, happy to let Dad handle it. Later on that evening I watched the news in the TV room on my ward. They were unable to shed light on the mystery of how a fifteen-year-old boy was shot by hunters in the same section of the Otways forest that police were pursuing the wild man known as Old Nick. As a minor, my name wasn't mentioned, neither was the crossbow wound to Bruce Botwin.

Amongst the stack of get-well cards, I saw one unsigned. It simply read, 'Get well son.' He was alive.

On Friday, I left the hospital for the first time with my left arm in a sling, accompanied by my father and the two detectives.

'Why me?' I asked Detective Bottomly in the car on the way out. 'Why not one of the others?'

He was in the passenger seat and he turned to me and said, 'The other boys have denied everything. Once we locate the body, we'll decide how to proceed.'

'And Nick … where is he? What's happening to him?' I'd already asked these questions on Wednesday.

'He's not our concern at the moment,' Bottomly said.

'Has he come in yet … has anybody spoken to him?'

'No one's seen him. At this stage he's no longer a part of our investigation. Don't want any more episodes of loose cannons running around the forest.'

Hayden was driving. He let a mild chuckle slip out, like my being shot wasn't an important event to him. 'Queensland Police are on their way down,' he said. 'We'll find him once this is all over. Any idea where he might be?'

I thought of the lonely house in the bush and knew exactly where he was hiding out. 'No. No idea.'

I led them down through the gully and found the grave. The entire area from the quarry right down past the creek was cordoned off with police tape. Four officers had followed in another car. Two were uniformed and carried shovels. The other two wore white overalls and carried large silver cases. I suspected they contained mobile laboratories of some sort.

Bottomly pointed at the grave. 'Ulsoo tryndigucrussearfust.' His speech became faster and if I didn't know better, I'd say he was excited.

I had no idea what he said but the officer with the shovel in his hand stared at Bottomly. 'You want me to dig across here first, yeah?'

'Aye man, whudryoowaitinfur.'

The officer began to dig across the top of the trench. I wondered what they were doing because the grave ran the other way. I'd told them that.

'It'll all be over soon, lud,' Bottomly said. Although I hadn't signed anything official, I trusted that he would live up to his word and look after me.

They took the first few easy shovelfuls out, then dug across and found virgin ground and established the wall of the grave. They repeated the exercise down the other end to allow them to outline the grave, and then began to dig up the loose soil. The other two officers sifted the dirt through a contraption with wire mesh. Every now and then, one or the other would hold up a piece of chewy or a butt and place it carefully in an evidence bag. Roddy and Soupy smoked relentlessly while we'd dug the grave, both times. My dad stood beside me, watching the whole time. The sun and the chill both dropped early in the forest, although it was only four o'clock in the afternoon. Soon the officers were standing waist deep in the trench and one officer pushed his probe in and put his weight onto it. It stopped at the point where I knew it hit the body. The officer gave Bottomly a weird look and nodded.

'Aye. Keep digging men.'

When the trench was deep enough the two forensic officers took over, working with smaller hand shovels. Dad and I watched on, his hand always on my good shoulder for support. Dad and I had always been a team and I needed him there with me, more than I knew. Finally the two officers slowed their work, until eventually they broke into a brief discussion of whispers. One called Bottomly over. The two constables and Hayden also accompanied the detective to the edge of the grave and peered down from on top. Then they all turned, glaring at me. Bottomly's eyes were full of hatred, I was sure of that.

'Lud, get over here.'

I didn't like his tone and didn't move.

Bottomly took hurried steps toward me, then reached out and grabbed my right bicep and squeezed.

'Get your hands off him,' my dad said.

Bottomly's cold, hard eyes showed anger. The fingers released, slowly. Dad's hand touched the middle of my back and forward we went, together.

'Luddy, doyathinkthusussumsortofajooke.' Spittle flew from his lips.

I stared at him, deciphering his words.

Jooke, Jooke? Joke. Shit! I looked into the trench to see the mass of dirty white wool, bulging eyes staring up. The sheep's tongue spliced between the frozen lips and blackened teeth.

CHAPTER 25

In the months afterward I'd catch Dad staring at his tomatoes a lot. Three, four, five times a day he'd check their colouring and make sure the bird net was working, but mostly I think he was just pondering. He slowed his drinking down and we put our house up for sale. Weekends were spent on long family drives through the countryside, searching for a town where we might be able to settle back down and start fresh. Tommy and I put our two bobs worth into the argument and asked if we could move to the beach. So we started looking down the coast and Mum fell in love with a little town called St Claire along the Great Ocean Road. Dad and I would start the business again.

I wasn't charged with giving a false statement. Perhaps being the victim of a gunshot wound actually saved me. Bottomly didn't believe my story of course, rather he believed I'd made it all up to get the police off Old Nick's trail and re-issued the warrant for his arrest. In one interview, he even told me he understood in some part why I was trying to cover for Nick, but then he went on to say he must be questioned and the law must deal with him because he was a fugitive. Nick became some sort of a notorious celebrity. Sightings were recorded across the country. According to different reports, he bought fuel in Broken Hill, groceries in Darwin and even walked into a picture theatre in Cooktown, far north Queensland. Every man and his dog thought they could go into the bush and find his shack. It became a tourist attraction, even after the Botwin brothers trashed it in revenge for Nick splitting Bruce's kneecap almost in half. Tony Debono's body was never found. I tried to tell Bottomly it had been buried a third time. Of course he didn't believe it and I couldn't blame him. Who would?

The happiest moment of my life came when I rode out and found Nick safe at that lonely house deep in the forest. I visited him every weekend and sometimes after school, as often as I could.

The owners of the house – the Joneses – operated a large engineering firm in Melbourne and helped Nick out tremendously. They knew he wouldn't do anything like what he was accused of and I met with them one day at the house. They listened to the whole bizarre story. I thought they'd hate me, but instead they were very understanding and believed me enough to hire Mr. Sandhurst, a big-time lawyer from Melbourne to represent Nick if he was caught. But the case became bogged down in both the courts and in the media as a test case for what is and isn't privileged information between a lawyer and his client. I read about it all in the paper. Nick also explained that the lawyer had decided he wanted to meet me, but not his client, Nick. That way he couldn't tell the authorities where Nick was because he didn't know.

Mr. Sandhurst came to the house on one occasion to meet me. Nick disappeared into the forest for the day. Mr. Sandhurst explained he wasn't going to use my story, rather he just wanted to know everything Bottomly knew, in case they had to prepare a defence.

It was reported in the paper that Mr. Sandhurst claimed he didn't even have to disclose who had hired him, as that party was not wanted for any criminal offence. He also argued that all he had to disclose was that he represented Nick Metaxas and this argument was still going on strongly through the media, while I put my head down and successfully completed my year nine studies.

As a family (including Tommy) we had a lengthy discussion on the events of the past months. I don't know if Tommy or my dad believed me, but later on I was to find out my mum certainly didn't believe any of my story. I also told them everything I could about Old Nick so they wouldn't worry about me when I disappeared for whole days. I didn't tell them where he was and they didn't ask. The wound to my left shoulder slowly healed and Dad, Mum and I cut a deal. If I passed year nine, I could begin my apprenticeship after Christmas and leave school behind once and for all. I knuckled down and studied hard, did all that homework and I think being shot helped me gain a bit of sympathy from my teachers, too.

I never spoke to my former mates again, but I spent these days paranoid for Rex. I knew Soupy was out there, somewhere in the darkness, waiting. I'd walk Rex before nightfall so he didn't have to go outside during the night. If he did, I followed. The police enlisted volunteers (my dad couldn't be involved of course) to search the surrounding forest for any evidence my story might have an ounce of truth, but they must have buried him much deeper in that forest.

In our street there might as well have been a great wall between the Debonos and us, and poor old Mr. Debono would never call me Mr. Gillings again. None of the other neighbours would speak to us either. Then came the removal of Father Graham Frost from our Parish, a week after school finished for the year.

When I look back on it, I think they skilfully slipped him out of town. Most people didn't find out for weeks later. We were told he was ill. A replacement priest from another town held Mass. I didn't go to that church again either because I would have had to face the Debonos. That's another deal I cut with my oldies, no more church. And Mum and Tommy drove to Beaconshire for Mass from then on.

I found out Father Frost had left via a different means. My intuition. Sometimes your mind sort of calls you and if you don't listen to it, you know you'll miss out on something major. The first time this happened to me was when I was young. I don't remember how young, but Tommy and I were watching cartoons when I saw Mum slip off into her room and close the door. An unusual thing for her to do in the middle of the morning. My mind summoned me. At the time I'd never done anything as bad as what I was about to do, and I can't imagine what my punishment would have been, had she caught me. I snuck into the kitchen and gently picked up the handset to hear Mum's voice on the other end talking to the dogcatcher. We had Yugoslavs living next door. They rented the Morrison's home for two years and I can't remember their name, but they had a German shepherd chained up full time and that thing barked like crazy most nights, keeping Tommy awake. Me, I'd stopped hearing it. Kind of like what fat Roddy said about living next to the train line.

Mum was telling the dogcatcher how she never saw them walk their dog or even let it off the chain, and how she wanted the council to come around and investigate them for animal cruelty. To my knowledge, nothing ever came of it and they moved out soon after. But I do remember the week before Christmas when my intuition summoned me to listen in again.

Dad had come home from the pub at around eight o'clock, the first Thursday night he'd been home early since I could remember. Except when we went on holidays. My brain was working in overdrive, calling me. I opened my bedroom door and heard them arguing in low voices in the kitchen and knew something serious was going on. I snuck down the hall and listened in.

'His tenure is finished, that's all. He's been shifted to another parish,' Mum said.

'He's been moved out of town, deliberately,' Dad said.

'I don't like your tone.'

'Yeah ... darl, listen. I don't know how to say this. They've found some writing in a scrabble book. Pictures too, hand drawn. Apparently Gina found 'em.'

Gina was Tony's mother.

There was a long pause. 'That boy ran away. This is filthy pub talk.' I imagined the strain on her screwed up, angry face.

Mum rarely mentioned Tony's disappearance to me again, and this was how I know she didn't believe my story, or *chose* not to believe it.

'It's true. Came from Bob Trellard,' my dad said.

Mr. Trellard was my math teacher.

'Who is also a Thursday night pisshead like you,' Mum snapped back.

'He knows what's going on ... knows what happened to the Holloway boy too. Reckons he took sleeping pills.'

Darren Holloway was the kid from my school that drowned in the river last year. I'd heard the rumours he'd taken sleeping pills, but they couldn't be true and why would he do that anyway? My school was full of rumours. That's another reason why I couldn't wait to get out of that weird joint.

'That boy drowned, everyone knows he couldn't swim. Father Frost is a good man. A priest, God damn you. I will not listen to any more of this.'

'Honey. I came home to tell you ... I want you to know what's going on—'

'Not from the pub I don't. Get ... just get ... go. Get back down there ... stay there for all I care. I'm going to bed.'

'I can't believe you. What if it's true? What if Tony threatened to expose him.'

'Father never would have done anything like that to a boy. No priest would.'

There was a long pause.

'Just go. Get out of my sight,' she said.

The back door slammed. I crept back to my room just in time to see Dad through the window, totally pissed and trying to ride my racer. He hit the fence, straightened up and took off. Mum went to bed, crying.

Our new priest, Father Rosdale had been introduced to our school a couple of weeks earlier. He seemed like a nice man.

By Christmas, the rumours about Father Frost being linked to Debono's disappearance had spread around. I couldn't help but think Meatlips and the boys were fuelling that story every chance they got.

As time passed, I couldn't stop questioning how I became involved in the burial process. Why didn't I listen to my mind back then? It was like a different person in the same body did that. I had done all I could in regards to disclosing the crime I'd committed, and if I wasn't to be believed, then I couldn't do any more. That's why I'm writing this. Someday someone will believe me. I still hear his neck crack and I know I'll regret my actions until my dying day. But I can't undo them, only own them. And I do.

CHAPTER 26

Once school finished I visited Nick nearly every day leading up to Christmas. With only the birds and Rex for company, we'd sit and talk beneath the pines and the gums, tend to his vegetables or play chess while my shoulder healed. I still couldn't beat him and he gave no quarter. He smashed through my defences by attacking constantly with his castles down either my left or right flank, but with every defeat I learnt more and soon enough, I worked him out. When I eventually cut off his flanking moves, I came up with a suicidal strategy of my own, which I secretly called, *get the bitch*. I noticed he gave me a look at his queen early on in each match, but he'd always taught me to play defensively. *Get the bitch* was an offensive strategy, the first plan I'd ever come up with. (It wasn't really a strategy, I just went full on and took whatever piece I could.) If I had a chance and there was a stand-off between our queens, I always took his off the board, happy to lose mine in return thinking I might have a show. So I began to swap queens, then bishops, horses and castles. The games moved faster, then on Christmas Eve I finally nailed him in checkmate. It was a momentous occasion in the hardest of years and I leapt up and danced around the room like an idiot. Old Nick laughed his guts out.

He couldn't surf and I know he was becoming increasingly frustrated at being cooped up in the house on his own. I took him books and cakes my mother made, eggs, lemons and tomatoes and we'd take long walks through the bush and fished in the river. The Joneses also visited once a fortnight and filled the freezer up. I knew he enjoyed my company, despite the problems I'd caused him. We had lengthy chats about everything and although he'd totally forgiven me, we both knew the lives we had before had gone forever, regardless.

On Christmas Day we went to my Uncle Laurie's for lunch and in the afternoon, I rode my ten-speed racer out with some left-over turkey and beef and a loaf of bread. Nick and I had our own little Christmas meal and a few games of chess. It was the best Christmas meal I'd ever had and I hoped it was the best he'd ever had too, because tragically, it was to be his last.

The next day I convinced him to watch the Boxing Day Test on TV. For a man who didn't like TV or cricket, he was totally glued to the telly as England won by three runs over five long days. I spent large parts of these days with Nick, but come dinner time, I'd hurry back to Bushmore because on the day after Boxing Day, the 27th of December, I met a girl named Wendy Schoenlepel. She was a skinny little thing with mousy ears poking through straight dark hair, who'd come down to spend the Christmas Holidays with her cousin, Dianne Harrington. I knew Dianne from primary school; she was a year above me. Wendy, as it turned out was also a year older. Apparently she'd been down visiting through the first term school holidays and seen me at the pinnies. She asked Dianne to introduce us, but according to Wendy, Dianne told her me and the boys were bad news.

This holiday, Wendy took it upon itself to move our one-sided relationship into a two-sided relationship. Groups of kids would often party at night down at the Emerald River in the picnic area beside the Wundowie Street bridge. Beneath the gums was a small patch of sand on the bank we called The Beach. Last year I'd been to a few of these summer parties and that's where I got drunk for the first time.

Word had gotten around I'd dobbed my mates in to the cops for killing Debono and, because no one believed me, I became a bit of a loner, an outcast. I couldn't wait to move out of that town. So when Dianne approached me one night at the pinnies – while I was on the KISS pinball machine – and introduced me to her shy cousin with the little speed hump titties, I was quite surprised.

The pinnies were a bit of a safe haven for me. Even though I often saw the other guys there, they wouldn't dare push me around inside the shop through fear of being barred. While I don't know what happened between them and the cops, I sussed they might also have been warned against having a go at me. Rex would lie just outside the front door where he could see me, providing that extra bit of security. He knew things weren't right with me.

I was chewing through my money on the machines, otherwise I looked like a deadbeat just hanging round there on my own. Cash was running low while my shoulder was healing. "You're about as useful as the one armed fisherman," Dad told me one time when we were laying aggie pipes. I knew he was only kidding, but that one cut to the bone a little.

'You going to the beach party tonight?' Dianne asked.

'Wasn't planning to. Haven't bought any grog.'

Wendy wore an eager look, smiling back at me. Hands tucked behind her back. I wanted to know what her voice sounded like. Her green eyes, with this black stuff around them, glanced away quickly. Dianne also wore the black stuff; I think they used pencils to put it on (Mum didn't wear makeup). She also made me nervous. I tried not to act frigid, even though I sussed that's exactly what I was, despite feeling like a bit of spunk at the same time.

'We've got champagne,' Dianne said. 'My boyfriend, Cam has some U.D.L.'s. Might give you one, if I ask.'

Your boyfriend? I looked at the cousin; she glanced away at nothing again. *That leaves you and me.* I let her know that telepathically.

"*She likes you,*" Dianne mouthed and threw her eyes back over her shoulder. Wow, that was totally unexpected.

'Okay. I'll come down. Have Meatlips and those guys been hanging down there?'

'Yeah … last night. But hey, no worries. I heard what happened. Everyone knows. But Cam's older, he'll make sure nothing happens to you.'

I cast a glance toward Wendy. She had not said one word.

'Couldn't give a stuff about 'em anyway,' I said. 'Meet you down there soon, yeah.'

'Just walk with us.'

So Rex and I did. It took about ten minutes to get down to the river and I walked my racer beside me, speaking to Dianne most of the way. My shyness meant I could only talk to the devil I knew. Last year, when I was fourteen none of the girls paid any attention to me at all. Now I was walking to a party with two sixteen-year-old chicks.

Wendy broke the ice. First words she ever said to me were, 'Heard you got shot?'

'What—?' Then I realised I hadn't thought about my shoulder since I'd met Wendy, only half an hour before. 'Oh … that was just an accident.'

'Heard it nearly killed you?' She had a surprisingly older voice. I liked it.

'No I'm okay, really, you don't have to—'

'Does it hurt … not getting shot … I mean … the wound, does it still hurt?'

I held my head a little higher. Being shot suddenly became a badge that might help me score here. 'Nah, it's right now.' Despite no longer having to use a sling, I carried my left shoulder with a slight drop in it and a constant bend in my elbow. Throbbing pain would visit me at night, although mostly through the days it felt like there was always a knot inside the muscle. Doctors said it would slowly go away as the muscles healed, but it felt like fragments of the bullet were still in there.

'What's it like—?' She stopped midway. I think Dianne might have touched Wendy's hand to silence her. I appreciated that because I was concentrating on walking my bike with one hand, the other was shoved in my jeans pocket trying to push my knob to one side. It was embarrassing me, pressing into my jocks and pitching like a tent. I hadn't even touched her yet, but the first girl to ever show interest in me was turning me on. Wendy changed the subject, 'Out of AC/DC, who's better, Bon Scott or that new guy?' It appeared she *wanted* to talk to me, and although it was nearly three years since he'd died, Bon Scott would always be the lead singer of AC/DC for me.

'Bon Scott was choice.'

Her smile gleamed. 'Reckon so. They'll give the new guy the arse soon.'

Wow. We had something in common. 'Reckon so too.'

'Me too,' Dianne said.

We arrived at the party around eight o'clock. They had a fire going and kids were swinging off a rope into the river. There was a small caravan park only a short distance up the bank where some of the kids were holidaying.

Sergeant Regowski had already visited earlier to make sure there weren't any underage kids drinking (which seemed rather stupid since if we were of age, we'd be at the pub). It was all a put-on. The cops preferred to know where we were drinking rather than having us go off lighting fires in the bush at night. Sergeant Regowski even allowed the fire pit to be dug in the sand close to the bank. Music had to be kept down after ten and turned off completely by eleven and once the cops had left, everyone retrieved their grog from the bushes. Wendy and I sat close to the warm glow of the fire, talking all night. I longed to touch her hand, just to find out how soft a girl's hand was, but didn't have the guts to do it yet. I hoped I wasn't permanently frigid.

Meatlips and the others lobbed about a half an hour after I arrived, but as we were with the older guys, they could only scowl at me. I tried to concentrate on Wendy but couldn't take my eyes off them. Not because I was worried, I just wanted to see their faces. I had a girl, an older girl and those morons had no chance when it came to chicks.

I took great joy in watching them sitting alone. How pathetic they looked. The girls must have thought so too as none were talking with them. A few of the younger kids hung around botting smokes off Soupy. The spikey mullet was longer and now hung straight down his shoulders, and fat Roddy – with pimples larger than his nuts – wore his stupid lumber jacket even in summer. His Fabergé stretch denims worked overtime. Meatlips and that spineless cretin Cudgy both wore their club jackets. They sipped pre-mixed grog from coke bottles, probably Bourbon or Southern Comfort. I was glad to be rid of them and their little club.

Cam was a good looking, friendly guy and I could see why Dianne liked him. He had this streaky fair hair; the same hairstyle as the little kid from the TV show, Eight is Enough. His mates were also good kids. They hung around the fire, dancing and singing to music, continually pumping out The Angels and AC/DC's Highway to Hell and a bit of Aussie Crawl. Wendy and I sang along to the words of every song. Cam took a breather from kissing Dianne and said to me, 'Heard what you did. Is it true?'

'Is what true?' I asked.

'Come on, man. Everyone knows what you told the cops.'

Wendy sat up straight. We'd been talking quietly, asking probing questions of each other while she patted Rex. He liked her straight away. Both of us had our legs crossed, our knees touching now. It was the closest we'd come to each other and all of a sudden the bored look washed from her face, and a questioning one arose as she listened.

'If I told you it's all true,' I said, 'would you believe me?'

'Don't know,' Cam replied. 'Certainly not what they say.' He nodded toward my former mates sucking on their large coke bottles, always watching me and no doubt talking about me too. 'They reckon you're full of crap.'

'Couldn't give a rat's arse what they say.'

'Word is, those arseholes want to beat the shit out of you.'

'Let 'em try.' I knew they wouldn't dare with the older kids around and they'd probably ruin the party too. I would be vulnerable on the way home in the dark though.

Being summer, Mum said I could stay out until ten o'clock. The more Wendy and I spoke and the closer we sat, the more I knew I'd be home late. I'd already decided that if she was allowed out later than me because of her age, then I'd have to nick off to find a phone and let Mum know. Wendy was smart and about to start year eleven and I really liked her. No way would I leave her here. I wouldn't be able to cope with the news if she'd gotten on with one of the other kids. I was also chewing over why she was interested in a boy a year younger than her. Cam had so many older mates hanging around who would have their licences and cars next year. As it turned out, luck was on my side and Wendy and Dianne also had to be home by ten, so Cam and I walked them to Dianne's house.

Cam and Dianne had been kissing all night, I guessed they'd probably had sex before too. All I had the nerve to do was work up the guts to hold Wendy's hand for the last five minutes of the walk home. She asked me to come horse riding the next day.

'I can't,' I said. 'Visiting a friend.' Oh I wanted to go horse riding of course. Wanted to spend every second I could with this girl, but I had to keep Nick company. It was my fault he was stuck in that house, and also I couldn't wait to tell him I almost had a girlfriend.

I arrived home twenty minutes late and Mum was surprisingly okay when I explained we'd walked some girls home. I'd stopped lying to them about everything, well almost everything. I told them I hadn't been drinking, but Cam gave me a U.D.L. vodka and passionfruit and told me I'd have to shout him one back.

The next day Rex and I rode out to see Old Nick. Rex had learnt to cut through the forest once I was out of sight and would meet me at the house. All I wanted to talk about was Wendy, my almost girlfriend. Must have bored the hell out of Nick, but he listened full on and my goal that night was to kiss her. Wendy and I hooked up at the pinnies and then wandered down to the party once more. I was happy to see Meatlips and the boys there because I also had another goal that night. I took a backpack with me and made sure they were watching when I pulled out my club jacket.

'What do you know, a LEE jacket,' I said toward them while I pissed on it. Then Cam and his mates all had their turn before I picked it up with a stick and tossed it on the fire. The girls were disgusted and it stunk a bit, but we laughed hard in the end. Soupy ran a finger across his throat in a hollow gesture aimed at me and a few baaaa noises floated on the air. That made me laugh at them even more. I don't think anyone else knew about the sheep.

Wendy returned a gesture of her own. First she gave me a passionate kiss on the lips, our first kiss, then she flipped Soupy the bird.

Afterwards we found a quiet spot to sit under the bridge on the concrete base of the pylon and kissed some more, our toes dipped in the current. Rex was hilarious. Once we started kissing he became jealous and squeezed in between us, making Wendy laugh like crazy.

'Do those kids worry you?' she asked.

'Nope.'

'You dobbed them in to the cops.'

'Stiff shit. No one believes me. Doesn't matter.'

She twirled the water with her foot. 'I believe you. You don't come across as someone who'd make stuff like that up.'

'That's all that matters then.'

'You know that makes you better than them.'

'I know. Thanks.'

'Yeah … and I called my boyfriend today too.'

I nearly fell into the water. 'What? You didn't tell me—'

'Dropped him over the phone, don't worry.'

'Oh … why?' It was a completely dumb question, but my mind was side-tracked by the boner I was desperately trying to keep down by my over-used powers of mental telepathy, and my elbow. I also wanted to hear the reason from her too.

'Because I want to be with you, silly.' She kissed me again and I grew so much I thought I might bust my zipper.

On the third day of my new life, I rode out to Old Nick's like I had a rocket beneath me. I couldn't wait to tell him for sure this time I *did* have a girlfriend. We watched cricket and played chess. I hadn't beaten him since I'd met Wendy and she was all I spoke about. He told me stories of his own situations with girls as a young guy back on the Gold Coast.

While I was at Nick's, her ex-boyfriend caught the train down from Melbourne that day and confronted her. Angry words were exchanged and the guy left and apparently went home.

Wendy and I were back under our bridge with the moonlight shining on the Emerald River when she told me all this. Unable to keep her wet lips off me, free as a bird. Then I heard some yelling behind us.

'I'm going to kick your arse!'

I turned to see this kid, a big kid pacing angrily toward us. Cam was running up behind him.

'Oh shit,' Wendy cursed. 'No Andy, don't!'

I figured it was her ex and stood up, ready to face him. Then Rex leapt in front of me, barking more savagely than I'd ever seen. The kid stopped in his tracks, not knowing if he was about to be attacked.

'You better piss off mate,' Cam said.

'Yeah. Who the fuck do you think you are?' Andy said and pushed him in the chest. Cam pushed him back but Andy realised he was outnumbered. Wendy jumped in between them and said, 'It's okay, Cam.'

'Back soon,' she said to me and led Andy down the river away from us. He shouted a hollow gesture at Cam, saying he was going to bring mates down from Melbourne in cars, but by that time Cam's mates were behind him and I think Andy must have realised he wasn't going to get Wendy back, no matter what. I felt sorry for him as he walked off down the riverbank, heartbroken.

I don't know what she said, but we didn't see him again and I hoped that would never happen to me. That year the school of hard knocks had taught me that you never know what's around the corner.

CHAPTER 27

Cam and I became good mates afterwards. I not only had a girlfriend, I also had a mate and at the time, that really was a big deal for me.

The next night I decided to leave Rex at home, luckily. I felt guilty. I hated leaving him behind because we were a team, but this was a girl and he had to learn not to get in the way. Wendy came prepared carrying her own little pink, blue and white striped beach bag. When darkness fell we moved away under the bridge. This time she led me by the hand a little further up the bank to a nice secluded spot in the long grass and pulled out a white and green checkered rug – neatly pressed like one of Mum's perfectly ironed tea towels – and laid it on the ground.

'Don't want to lie on the grass,' she said.

Her legs were tanned, ending somewhere mysterious above her canary yellow skirt. I thought of sex, although I had no idea of how to broach the subject and if she'd do it at all. I'd planned on buying condoms, but Mum's church friend Mrs. Cottee ran the pharmacy and I knew the minute I walked in with that – *I want to buy condoms* – guilty look on my face, she would hunt me down and serve me herself. I was going to ask Cam at some stage, but my goal for the night was to work up the guts just to put my hand down her top, if she'd let me.

'What do you do during the day?'

I knew a question like this was coming because she'd rang through the day and asked my mum if I could come down to the surf beach with her family.

'Just stuff.'

'What kind of stuff? Your old lady sounded like she had no idea where you were.'

'Just stuff … can't say.' I couldn't tell her about Old Nick. No one could know where he was.

'Is it to do with what happened?'

I was falling for a mind reader. 'Yeah.'

'Show me … your shoulder? Show me?'

She was already lifting up my tee shirt and I took it off. Wendy studied my wound, which looked like a round, brownish reddish blot of scar tissue under the moonlight. She ran two fingers over it. 'That man … the bush man you were protecting, you know where he is don't you?'

'How do you know?'

'Everyone says you're strange, and the answers you give me tell me you're hiding things pretty deep.'

I rolled her over and kissed her, then whispered, 'He's my best friend, besides you. I tell him everything I can about you.'

'But you can't tell me about him?'

'Nope.' I could feel her nipples against my chest, as hard as little river pebbles and her breath, hotter than the afternoon air of the day. I kept my hand on her waist wanting to move it up. Or down.

Her smile broke open. 'I'm on the pill. Let's do it.'

'Do What?' My idiot of a mouth asked. Perhaps I had to make sure of what *it* actually was. Of course I knew what she meant by *it,* but *it* made me scared … and hard. Harder and more scared than ever before. Wendy didn't answer, just took over and unzipped me. I caught the top of the inside of my shorts and feared I'd explode before she could wrangle it free, but wrangle it free she did. My hand hadn't even found her breasts before she pulled down my shorts and totally guided me inside seconds later. She was as wet as a stream and I lasted about three seconds and became a man on the 30th of December 1982. You never know what's around the corner but it costs nothing to look. All of a sudden life was off and running again.

She invited me to Dianne's place for a New Year's Eve barbeque. They lived on a farm a couple of miles out of town to the north where Wendy kept her horse, Charcoal. I'd never been near a racehorse and I was gobsmacked at its extraordinary beauty, a coat of the shiniest colour of black imaginable. Charcoal looked down at me, like I was inferior. When I saw those rippling muscles and the tracking veins beneath its skin, I knew then I wanted to own a racehorse one day.

Wendy's mum, Dot was a big blonde woman with a tattoo of a rose on her left shoulder. Her dad, Hans was an even bigger Dutchman, six and a half foot at least, with a bullbar moustache. He wore Stubbies shorts and a blue singlet, like the ones you always see truckies wear. He also had wild, light and curly shoulder length hair and faded tattoos on his biceps and forearms. Attached to his wrists were hands that could wrap around my head as though it were a cricket ball.

Dianne's parents were a little mellower, drinking red and white wine, but Hans was well drunk by the time we arrived. I think he told me about a dozen times during the night, that he'd chucked the lamb on the spit around two in the afternoon when he'd come home from the pub, and kept drinking since. I also learnt many times that night, Schoenlepel was Dutch for shoehorn. I liked him. Guess I had to because his arm was around me a lot, swamping me with the breath of a thousand wet dogs, and tobacco. He let me drink his beer and cooked the most amazing homemade bratwurst sausages I'd ever tasted, and we ate all night beside a raging fire. A rusty, claw foot bathtub on the verandah was full of VB cans on ice. I thought an army might have been coming, but no, just the neighbours and drop-ins who came and went through the night.

Hans was a great guy, the type to get along with anyone who'd share a beer. Although, I was on the lookout for his dark side, which I figured might be exposed the second he found out I'd screwed his daughter. Sometimes when I was talking, he'd lean forward, staring at the ground with a serious face, making weird grunting sounds while nodding his head. I soon worked out (when I saw him do it to other people) that's how he concentrated because he was so pissed.

'Dad says you can stay the night,' Wendy said, around ten o'clock. I'd been wondering how I was going to get home. I'd already had two cans and wasn't going to have any more, in case I had to call Mum to come and get me.

'Where'll I sleep?'

'My room ... you okay with that?'

I stared at her, then at Goliath as he skulled another can, crushed it and chucked it in the fire. She must have seen the fear in my eyes because she said, 'Just kidding. Dad said he'd set up tents in the back yard for you and Cam. He's pretty cool about it all.'

"It all." What did she mean by *"it all?"* Did Hans know what *"it all"* really meant?

'I have to call my oldies first.' Mum said I had to be home straight after midnight. 'You got a phone?'

'Follow me.' She led me into the kitchen and I rang Mum, hoping she'd be home. They hadn't told me they were going out and Mum would not appreciate me leaving a message telling her that I was staying at my girlfriend's home. Luckily she answered and I explained what was going on.

'Can I speak to her father?' Mum asked.

My shoulders slumped. No way. This guy had drunk a river and for a brief second I thought it might be better that our mums speak, then I heard Wendy's mum outside cackling her wild laughter and called out, 'Hans ... can you come talk to my mum?'

'Sure,' he said. That bullbar moustache widened like the jaws of a vice to frame the largest grin I'd ever seen on a man. He grabbed the phone. 'Hello.' His voice sobered, his face took on a serious mode, oozing responsibility while listening, staring at the floor, concentrating. 'It's fine. No problem at all, Mrs—'

—

'Mrs. Gillings.'

—

'Yes.'

—

'It's a beautiful night.'

—

'Delightful.'

—

'Oh yeah, stars are out.'

—

'Uh huh.'

—

'Nope, jober as a sudge.'

—

'Only kiddin … the two boys can sleep outside in tents.'

—

'Yep, I'll make sure and I'll run him home in the morning for you.' He listened some more while nodding and making faces at me. I cringed, but Mum bought it all.

'Okay, don't worry bout a thing. He's in good hands.'

—

'Happy New Year to you Mrs. Gillings.' He gave me the thumbs up. The big hand covered the mouthpiece and he nodded toward his own wife and said, 'If I can handle that woman over there, mate I can handle any woman.' Then he started up that crazy, snorting laughter.

I had to force myself to stop cracking up before I spoke to Mum again.

'He sounds like a really nice man, honey. When can we meet this girlfriend of yours?'

'Tomorrow, I'll bring her round in the morning.'

'Sounds nice, honey. Happy New Year.'

'Happy New Year, Mum.' And it was done. Now I could relax and enjoy my first New Year's Eve away from my parents. I reached into the bathtub and pulled out a beer. Hans and Dot seemed to laugh at anything remotely funny and at one stage in the night, the fact that Wendy hardly let go of my hand became a source of their amusement. Just before midnight, Hans passed on some of his memorable advice. 'Don't marry your first girlfriend,' he bellowed. 'I did, look what I ended up with.'

Laughter followed, but Dot thumped him across the chest and said, 'Had a dozen decent one's before 'im ... thirteen's unlucky, huh.' And then her broad cackling carried across the night once again.

New Year's came faster than me the night before. Hans let off some fireworks and I saw them sparkle in Wendy's eyes as we kissed each other long. The party fizzed out around two o'clock. Cam and I set up our tents and finally, after six full cans of beer – more than I'd ever drunk before – I crashed in my tent, only to be woken a short time later with hair in my face. I looked up to see Wendy, naked with her finger on her lips.

'Shhhh.'

I was as quiet as a mouse as she slipped into the sleeping bag. I wanted to mention to her there was a guy in the house that would probably roast me on the spit tomorrow for this, but of course I didn't and we played with each other for a couple of hours until she snuck back inside. It was the most terrifying, pleasurable sex and I learnt fast that Wendy had a thrill seeking, adventurous side to her. I also heard groans from the tent next door and knew Cam and Dianne were into it too. A song hummed away in my head, Jack and Dianne by

John Cougar. It had been my favourite song through the year, (along with Waiting For a Girl Like You by Foreigner) and we'd even played it earlier that night with Hans and Dot, arm in arm singing along with Dianne's parents and all the neighbours. I wondered if that song was some type of an omen and if I was supposed to be with Dianne instead. But when Wendy wrapped her legs around me and bit into my earlobe, I knew there was no mistake. Still, I couldn't get that damn song out of my head.

CHAPTER 28

Our house wouldn't sell. So Dad decided to give it a fresh coat of paint and replaced the old hardwood windows with cedar frames. We all chipped in and helped, including Wendy. One day while we were still painting, the agent rang to take some people through. Dad was reluctant because the place was a mess but the salesman insisted. I remember the day specifically because the agent took the people around the back as Mum let out a loud scream. Everyone ran to the front and she told us how she was painting beside a window, when a white cockatoo landed and bit off a chunk of cedar. We all laughed, so did the purchasers who offered a thousand less than the asking price. We met them half way and dropped five hundred bucks, then bought an old fifties fibro house in St Claire and set the moving date for the eighteenth of March.

Everything was going to plan. I started my apprenticeship with Dad and juggled what time I had left between Wendy and Nick. He let me bring Wendy to the house one day, so we rode Charcoal out. He was stoked to meet her, and of course he trusted me when I told him she wouldn't say a word about him to anyone, and she didn't.

Dad and Hans became mates. They were often seen having a few beers together through January and on one warm Saturday night, they were in the pub. Wendy and I were smooching on the bench seat out the front of the pinnies, amongst a group of other kids. She wanted me to walk her home and I told her to hang on for a minute.

It was dark, around nine thirty. I'd seen Lenny Botwin's car cruising past the pub, twice in the past fifteen minutes. He was out on bail. We waited and he came back and parked, then walked into the pub with two of his older brothers. I couldn't take my eyes off the door because my dad was also a guy you don't want to mess with. He'd told me what'd happen if he ever saw Lenny again and I'd heard stories of Dad going off in his younger days. I watched the door. The glass was tinted so we couldn't see what was going on inside the pub from the other side of the road. We heard a crunch, the door shook, then another crunch. The glass cracked. The door opened and Lenny came tumbling out beneath the streetlight, blood pouring from his forehead. Dad was right behind him and rammed him into the phone booth in front of the pub, breaking the glass in that, too. Then he kept hitting him in the same spot on the forehead. I think Lenny might have been unconscious by then. His legs were wonky and Dad was holding him up at arm's length, not saying a word, no yelling, just punching. Bodies spilled out the door to watch. Big Hans stood with his back to my dad, grinning and staring Bruce and Frankie Botwin down. Neither of them dared raise a hand. The police came within minutes and dragged Dad off Lenny and by that time, my dad was finished with him. They were the older guys in the town and that's how they settled everything. Normally they'd have a beer afterwards and carry on like nothing happened, but not this time and to my knowledge the Botwins didn't come back to the pub until we left town. Dad told me later Lenny tried to apologise for accidentally shooting me.

Wendy went home at the end of January. After so many passionate nights and days where we found every moment we could to be together, I became worried about our relationship. I knew from the first time we met, this romance might die when she went back to her city life that I had little knowledge of. She was so pretty. I figured there was a good looking rich boy on every corner in Melbourne. My world was empty, and while she told me she wouldn't go near her ex-boyfriend again, I spent many hours of broken sleep stressing out and made sure we spoke on the phone every evening. Earning a wage meant I could also make plans to catch the train to Melbourne on weekends, although I was yet to have a Saturday off because Dad and I had heaps of work to finish before the move. I longed to take her out and spend my pay at some posh city restaurant.

Wendy went back to school on the first week of February, and then on the sixteenth, she had what was called a curriculum day. I'd never heard of a curriculum day, we didn't have them at my school. Those bastard Christian Brothers wouldn't hear of a day off school. But apparently curriculum days were held so her teachers could have a bunch of meetings. Sounded like a con to me, but all that mattered was Wendy rang a couple of days before and told me her dad was bringing her down for Tuesday night and Wednesday. The weather forecast predicted forty-one degrees and a Total Fire Ban was issued across the state, so Dad and I also took Wednesday off. We'd already had a couple of hot days nudging forty degrees that February.

Hans turned out to be an easy-going type of guy and was okay with us sleeping together. I'd stayed over several times through January. Wendy and I woke to a balmy sunrise and by mid-morning, the stinking hot northerlies kicked in. We rode Charcoal down to The Beach after lunch to swing off the rope and swim in the river, with no one to bother us. Not long after that, maybe around three o'clock, the first of the fire trucks – sirens blasting – sped over the Wundowie Street Bridge above our heads. I had planned on joining the C.F.A. with Dad, but he told me to wait until my shoulder was fully healed and we had moved to St Claire. We climbed up the bank and could see the smoke billowing up in the distance to the south.

'Let's go take a look,' Wendy said.

I wasn't too keen. I knew the danger of bushfires and this year, there had been many large fires around Victoria. A lot more than usual. But Wendy infatuated me with those green eyes, the tilt of her head and that smile. I'd do anything for her so we hopped on Charcoal and headed out along the Coast Road toward the blaze until we reached a roadblock. I couldn't smell the smoke because the wind was at our backs, but it looked a big fire. Fred Courtney, one of Dad's C.F.A. mates was on the roadblock. 'It's a grass fire,' he said.

'Where's my dad?'

'He's with the crew setting up containment lines to the south.'

'How big is that fire?' I was worried. If he was on the south side, that meant he would have forest at his back and I knew how dry it was out there. If the fire took hold, it would sweep through the bush fanned by the strong northerlies behind it. Dad could be in trouble.

'Just a few paddocks at the moment,' he said, 'we've got it well contained. There's a westerly change coming in soon anyway. Might bring rain with a bit of luck. Safest place for you two is in town.'

We headed back up the road, but Wendy was gripped with excitement. She stopped the horse and turned as far as she could in the saddle to face me. 'I want to see the fire. Take me closer … pleeease?'

'I can't. If that change comes through and ends up coming in from the south, it could head towards town.'

'Oh come on. I've never seen a bushfire before.'

The temperature had risen dramatically in the last hour. I'd never experienced a hotter day. The air was stifling, almost unbearable. I knew it was well over forty degrees. The horse had broken into a lathering sweat. 'Wendy, this is not a game—'

'Pleeease?' Those pretty eyes bulged and pleaded. She grabbed my cheeks and gave me a passionate kiss and at the end, she latched onto my bottom lip and bit firm enough to hold on.

'Thake meeee cwosaaaa,' she muffled, giggling as her teeth clung on. I tried not to laugh back, fearing she'd bite harder and cause a cold sore to spring up. I hadn't told her about my embarrassing disease because I hoped it had disappeared. I hadn't had a cold sore since the winter of 1981.

'Owwwight, owwwight,' I muffled back and she let go.

'Take me, take me, take me. You promised.'

'Wendy, stop farting around. We really got to get out of here. You heard those guys, it could come this way.' But then I got an idea, a particularly pleasing one. 'We could go to the quarry and watch it from there.' We weren't far away and the quarry was elevated above the surrounding bush where the valley dropped. It would be safe there and we'd be able to see the fire.

'The quarry? Where's that?'

'Come on, I'll take you.' We had thin bush to our right and I took her down a gully track leading to the quarry. We tied Charcoal at the gates. There was a police sign warning trespassers would be prosecuted and the gate was still chained up.

'How do we get in?' Wendy asked.

'Simple.' I grabbed the chain and pulled hard, it fell loose. I knew the boys would have cut it by now and chained it back to look like no one could get through, and in we went.

I climbed the ladder with a grin from ear to ear. The charter of the Bushmore Motocross Club was still written on the wall. If not for Wendy, I would have pissed on that too. I read the first rule.

Rule 1: No girls.

I was thinking about how cool it would be to have sex up here and how I'd let them know somehow, when I saw a stick mag in one corner. I quickly tossed it out the side window before Wendy poked her head through the opening. She took a look around.

'What the hell is this place?'

I told her about the club and how I used to ride with those wankers, even about winning their stupid inaugural title. In the distance we could see the smoke, thick and black, turning the sky into a brown haze over the treeline of the gully where we'd originally buried Debono. The season had been busy for fire-fighters, but the C.F.A. had cleared fire trails early in spring and I hoped their containment lines would hold. Far off to the east where Nick was hiding out in the house, we saw only blue skies. I wrapped Wendy in my arms and started kissing the back of her neck.

'You're not thinking of having sex here, are you?'

'Would be kinda nice.'

'You kidding me? Who knows what you hard up fifteen-year-old boys do in here. You think I didn't see what you threw out the window.' I grinned and couldn't argue with her. We watched the fire for a while until she got bored and we did it standing up, anyway. Guess it's a woman's prerogative to change her mind.

With a piece of shale, I scratched a love heart and our names over the rules of their club and we left the Bushmore quarry for the last time. We had to shield our eyes from the whirling dust as we rode home into those fierce northerlies. Back at the farm, Hans told us of the devastating fires that had taken hold across Victoria and South Australia, sweeping through hundreds of thousands of acres. Houses were lost and many were feared dead. The Dandenong Ranges to Melbourne's east and Mount Macedon to the north were ablaze.

I called Mum. She answered on the first ring and told me she'd only just heard from Dad. He was okay and they had the fire under control for now, but there was still a severe weather warning. She ordered me home. Wendy and her dad left for Melbourne and I raced to Pinehurst Avenue to be with Mum and Tommy. We watched the news. She sat crying as the full extent of the fires took hold. Ash Wednesday, they were already calling it. The worst bushfires in Australia's history were right on our doorstep. We packed the car ready to flee in case the evacuation order came through. Until then, all we could do was sit and wait for the cool change, not knowing the full extent of what was happening to the south. The change arrived. Our new windows shook from what we thought at the time were welcoming cooler winds from the west. They howled through like never before. The sky to the south blazed a dusty orange, there was no sunset that day.

Dad arrived home at three in the morning, battle wearied. Every line and pore in his exhausted face was filled with ash and grime. What we thought was a bushfire, he described as an inferno, hotter than hell. We listened in horror as he described the blindness, the choking air, the sound of the raging firestorm was like jet engines, as the normally cool westerly's blasted through at over a hundred knots under the cruellest hand of nature imaginable, creating a furnace-like atmosphere. A front many kilometres wide burned east out of control, razing everything in its path. Fire-fighters and residents were forced to flee as it obliterated towns along The Great Ocean Road, unhindered. Houses exploded in front of him, debris filled the air. Helpless, they were forced to retreat and could only watch it burn out at the ocean.

I couldn't imagine a sound like jet engines. For the second time in under a year, I didn't have the capacity to fully understand. I'd never flown in a plane before and the south westerlies were meant to be a saviour and bring cooler weather. Some of the early reports said the fire was believed to have reached nearly two thousand degrees Celsius. I struggled to believe that, but apparently it was true.

'Nick,' I said. 'He's out there.'

I watched my dad's distraught face tighten. 'Where?'

I told him where the house was.

He shook his head. 'Shit … how do you know he's there?'

'It's where he's been hiding out.'

He sighed, but I knew his heart was heavy. 'Lots of people escaped, mate.'

'I have to go.'

'Where? There's … there's nothing there anymore.'

He was right. The futility struck me. Nick would have gotten out for sure. Still, I stressed about him and laid on the couch next to Dad holding back tears. He caressed my hair until I fell asleep. I woke at the breaking dawn in a panic to the reliable calling of my mind.

He's dead, he's dead.

I lifted my head, the wall clock said half-five. A horrible, bleak, haze-filled morning approached over our corner of the Otway Ranges. My exhausted father snored.

Old Nick did not escape. I tried to block the thought. Maybe he'd driven out and made it to farmland, north of the forest's edge, but I couldn't stop thinking of what Dad had said. *"A front, miles wide"*. The house was smack in the middle of the forest and he wouldn't be there if not for me.

I told myself over and over that he'd escaped, still I ran out to my motorbike and fled down along Whispering Creek and out to the Coast Road, leaving Rex to try as best he could to make his own way. I headed east, tearing through the abandoned dirt roads until I reached a fire truck parked sideways. Another roadblock.

I detoured through the blackened, smouldering bush and dead valleys, dodging roo and wallaby carcasses. I came out onto another road lined with open fields of dead livestock on my left. Yesterday's green forest to the right was now eerily black and silent. My mind recalled the darkest corners, thin snippets of sleep where I'd dreamt of army tents, dishevelled survivors, me turning their shoulders looking for Old Nick in a place I knew he wouldn't be, couldn't be. Deep in the forest I reached the Turnbull Track, a grey, charred ruin of trees as black as Charcoal's coat to either side. I raced along, passing the stump that like everything else, no longer existed. I knew Nick was gone. Tears streaked parallel to my ears. What had I done?

I reached the house. Smoke lifted from ash ruins. No timber, no windows, no birds, no life, no wind, only cinders, buckled roof iron and black peace. No one could have survived.

Nick got out. Nick got out. I kept turning the thought over and over. The shed was another heap of ash, settled like snow. I ran over to see the back end of the tailgate, the shell of Nick's Holden beneath the twisted iron, the front driver's side door wide open. I peered in to see a blackened figure, tiny, beside another and another and another figure on the charred floor. More soot covered chess pieces sat in their neat arrangement where a box had been once, keeping them for all the time Nick had possessed them. He had tried to leave, and he had tried to take his chess set with him because he would never have left without those pieces. I fell to my knees and cried, yelling his name time and again to no one as a hunk of smouldering, dead plant singed the skin on my knee. I wanted to feel it sear; I deserved pain, I deserved to die instead of Nick and pushed harder into the scorched earth, wanting myself to burn as I searched the pillars of black wood, a desolate landscape knowing he would have tried to run once the fire turned, knowing he would always be out there. Knowing I had killed my best friend, Old Nick.

THE END

EPILOGUE

The knock on the door was not as terrifying as I thought it would be. Not as terrifying as when I saw her at Jack's funeral. Unexpectedly.

I opened it. 'Angela. Come in.' She stepped in through the front door wearing a white shirt-top beneath a navy suit, a matching long skirt and stockings. Young Tony Debono's sister, the girl I once knew from down the road had grown into a beautiful lady, mature, powerful. Every bit the lawyer. Her heels hollowed a dominant sound on the timber floor.

'Thank you, Mr. Gillings.'

'Please, call me John. Have a seat.'

'John.' She smiled, but instead turned and walked to the front window, gazing out over Bass Strait and the St Claire Golf Club. The manuscript tucked beneath her arm.

'Jack's name was John too,' I said. 'We just called him Jack, you know.'

'I heard that at the funeral. Never knew, not too many in Bushmore would have. Did he play golf?'

'Played off nine, which they tell me is pretty good.'

'It is,' she said. 'I play too.'

At the funeral we spoke briefly. I was saddened when she told of how her parents, Tony and Gina both died in the last decade within a few years of each other, broken-hearted. Her father was my friend. I missed him a lot when we moved out of Bushmore. I told her of the death of my own wife three years ago. She spoke to my youngest son, Tommy for a short time and left. Next day I contacted her law firm, told her what Jack had given me and couriered the manuscript up.

'This is his house?' she asked.

'His beach house. He lived on the other side of Melbourne.'

'Stunning. Very architectural … but boxy with no eaves. Why don't they use eaves anymore?'

'Who knows. Not my style either. Local guy designed it. Difficult fella, but did a great job.' I shrugged. 'You know … architects.'

'Tell me about it. My husband and I are building at the moment. What did it cost to build something like this?'

I winced. Why did she want to know that? She stared at me from the other side of the room, wanting an answer.

'Think he said a couple of mill.'

'Bricks … I heard you say at the funeral.'

'Bricks.'

Despite this somewhat uncomfortable conversation, I chuckled at the memory, and said. 'That was the way Jack spoke when it came to money. A gorilla was a thousand, a brick a million.'

'Looks like Jack made a lot of bricks in business.'

I wondered if this was about money.

'He did all right. Went to work for a mate of mine in Melbourne on multi-storey buildings when he finished his apprenticeship with me.'

'I backed one his horses in a Melbourne Cup,' she said. 'Mr. Majestic. Ran fourth. Didn't know it was his until later on. Then I followed several of his horses. It was exciting watching them come home, knowing they were Jack's.'

It seemed a strange comment, after what she now knows of Jack. I assumed she'd read it all. 'Wendy got him into horses. They owned a stud farm. Me, I was happy to sit in the pub and watch the races. Jack being Jack, had to be a part of it all. Used to go trackside and watch them run trials early in the morning. He'd ring me and say "put the house on this thing Dad, it's running like shit out of a shanghai." I think Jack was right, perhaps I did get that saying wrong.'

'Yeah.' She chuckled. Her smile was warm. She'd been very comforting at the funeral, despite everything. Now she was still compassionate, even after reading Jack's manuscript, "Enough Rope". A little too compassionate, maybe, almost like there was a glow about her. She gazed around the room. 'I was blown away by Tommy's speech, how Jack made supervisor at twenty-two, partner at twenty-nine. Overseas contracts. Turned the business into the one of the largest plumbing companies in Australia.'

'So they say.'

'Sailed in Sydney to Hobarts, didn't he own that Maxi-yacht?' She clicked her fingers.

'The Dog House. He part-owned it.'

She smiled. 'How could I forget that name? Who would call a boat that?'

'Reckons Wendy sent him there a few times, he also loved his dogs. He had a weird sense of humour. Guess where he got that from.' I looked at the manuscript and had to ask. 'You read it?'

'Cover to cover in a day. Then I read it again. Brought back so many memories, good and bad, but it was thirty-two years ago.'

'I'm sorry ... really I am.' I fought back tears. What did she think of my family?

She came and sat next to me. My hands trembled. She held them, firm. 'It's not your fault, John. It's not Jack's fault either.'

'What do you mean? You read it. I should have taken him fishing ... spent more time with him, instead of all that drinking. You read the bit where he said he kicked Tony and heard his neck crack. My son killed your brother.' I couldn't fight the tears back anymore, they spilled down my cheeks. 'My boy killed him.'

She tightened her grip. 'He might have already been dead. There's nothing we can do. They're both gone now ... we'll never find his body, but this is evidence. It's like a death bed confession.'

She surprised me. 'Against who … those other boys?'

'Maybe, but they're not important to me either. Don't you understand, we can release this. In a way I never would have dreamt, Jack has confirmed what we always knew. You see back then, no one would talk to our family either about Father Frost. We knew what he did to Tony. We found drawings, notes; he even wrote a letter to himself when he was twelve. Posted it, received it and opened it, such was his torment to want to tell someone. But without a victim we couldn't bring it to trial.'

I wiped my eyes, still a little unsure where she was heading. 'This doesn't prove anything, either.'

'Do you know of my work?'

'Yes.' Her law firm handled many child abuse cases relating to the church.

'It doesn't have to prove anything. It is what it is. My life's work has been about prosecuting these people who I know harmed my brother. Turns out I've been working in the wrong court. I know a writer, we can use Jack's words in the court of public opinion and that's where they're losing the war. We just need it to make a statement, that's all. They make me sick, those cardinals and bishops in their ivory towers. Men appointed to powerful positions within the Vatican, yet can't remember the documents relating to hush money they paid victims. They stink of lies and dirty money they throw at their barristers. Society is foolish to think and hope they will one day tell the truth. Rest assured, that will never happen but the good news is we are heading in the right direction. When I grew up the priest was beyond question, now, they're still beyond question for the wrong reasons, they're too scared to front the inquiries. Society has changed its thinking, they are no longer the untouchable men of God. One of my early clients was the family of Darren Holloway. You remember, the boy who took the sleeping pills and drowned. They sued the school and lost. We knew he was a victim of Brother Hobbins, but there's no proof.'

'So, what ... are you thinking of prosecuting them over this?'

'No. Don't you see, we can print it. We can do more damage by publishing it as a story. We can't beat them in the courts or the Royal Commissions. They sit there in all their robes and their golden rings, using their godly manner to say they can't recall anything through their gold-capped teeth. They're delusional old men who think God chose them to represent him. Why would a God choose such creeps who moved their slimy priests around for decades, knowing they were hiding their crimes? Hiding their wolves in sheep's clothing, shuffling them around from parish to parish, state to state, they even moved them overseas. It happened worldwide, an international, well organised crime against humanity. Thousands of lives ruined. If they told the truth, they'd be opening themselves up for global prosecutions. They crunched their numbers decades ago and knew of dwindling stocks coming into the priesthood. There were so many bad apples, if they turned them over to the police, they wouldn't have anywhere near enough priests left to go around. They're too smart, too slippery and have stockpiled a war chest to fight us. Can you believe the Vatican has even set up their own council to investigate these priests? To punish them under Canon law.'

'Hang on a minute. They're the ones who hid them in the first place.'

'Kind of like asking your drug dealer to help with your rehab, huh. This way, they can't answer to it because again, they'd only open themselves up. Silence is their weapon. They're very professional when it comes to releasing well-spun statements, then answering no further. Society has given them enough rope. They've had their opportunity to come clean. If this goes to print, it doesn't matter what they say. It's a true story.'

'What about the names?'

'We'll change what we need to. You won't recognise it when I'm finished.' Her face lit up. 'John, don't you see, I've never been more excited about anything. I can do more with this than I can with the statements of a thousand victims.'

I gazed at this brave woman who should be mourning her brother, she could only see a brighter light. 'My money went into that church.'

'Mine too, for a few years until I woke up,' she said, 'and my parents' money. Straight into the coffers of old men who paid the lawyers. Frost did a few years. We got him on the testimonies of boys from another parish back in the sixties. Rosdale, the priest who replaced him in Bushmore turned out to be one of the state's worst offenders. He'll never get out of jail.'

'I read all about it.'

'Like so many of them, Frost blamed celibacy.'

'Could've just gone down the knock shop and got his rocks off. No one would have known the difference.'

'I wouldn't have put it quite like that, John, but those types of men should never be allowed near children, yet they're left alone to run entire schools. Their actions caused one boy to became a bully, and another to think that taking sleeping pills and floating down the river was the only way out to escape their clutches. This way they don't get off for what they did to those two boys.

'You see, back then I noticed the change in Tony too, around grade five and six. We were very close before that, I loved him like a normal sister loves her little brother. He was a typical boy. Sure we had the odd fight here and there, the odd argument, but he turned and made my life miserable. He became mean, introverted, alienated from us, his family. How does a boy cope with when a mongrel he trusted – our family trusted – does something like that to him? He was just a kid. Jack noticed the change too. All of Bushmore's dark secrets are in here.' She tapped the manuscript.

'Through our teenage years I hated my brother. I wanted him gone, slept at a friend's house as often as I could. I'd come home to find my room trashed for something as little as an argument he couldn't let go of. He was brutal toward me, said things a brother should never say to a sister. Said horrible things to my mother too. Dad was the only one who had any control over him. I've never told this to anyone but I must confess, at the time I was sorry he was gone as my brother, but not as a person, if you can understand that. Jack saw his nasty side too. It's all related back to what the priest was doing to him when they were altar boys. None of us knew. We're all victims.'

'That's why you do this work?'

'I can't turn my back. Tony will always be my brother. After everything we've found out since he died and after reading this, I've learnt to still love him. But there's another aspect to this. I moved to Melbourne to study law at nineteen. The only two priests I knew in that town were Frost and then Rosdale. Bushmore had a one hundred per cent failure rate. You can take different views. You can ask what are the odds of that happening, or you can accept how widespread it really was. I've travelled the length of this country and my work tells me the latter is true.

'Now we can do so much more.' She rubbed my hand. 'Why did you give it to me, the manuscript?'

'Because of who you are ... and your work. But I may not have if I hadn't seen you at the funeral. Once I spoke to you, I realised it's your right to know.'

'Thank you. It's closure for me.'

'He asked me to destroy it after I read it.'

'Why didn't you?'

'Because I'm his father. I make the decisions for this family.'

She gave me this long questioning look. Tears welled in her eyes, lips parted eventually forming a delicious smile, then she rocked back in the seat, shaking her head gently, almost laughing and crying at the same time.

I sat back too. 'What?'

'You don't know about the email?'

'What email?' I asked, surprised.

'The day before Jack died I received an email from his office. He requested me to attend his funeral.'

'He requested—? Jack was in hospital.' Then I thought aloud. 'Linda.'

'Linda's signature was on the email. A lady named Linda Shaw.'

I nodded. 'Jack's secretary. It appears he gave one more instruction.'

'It appears so, John. If I didn't know better, I'd say this meeting was meant to take place.'

'If I didn't know better, it appears he's still making decisions from the grave.'

'Your son was a very astute man. I think he's telling us he knew about all the cases. He knew the full impact those men had on Bushmore. On Tony ... and I suppose on himself, too.'

I shook my head in disbelief. My son was testing me, still. I looked at the manuscript, his legacy. Long moments passed before I heard a chair grind and dishes being stacked in the kitchen.

'You ready for that game, old man?' Nick called out.

'Not yet mate. We got company. You got a second?'

'Sure.' Nick entered the room.

'Meet Angela Debono,' I said. An ... an old friend of mine and ... I guess Jack's too.'

She nodded briskly. 'It's Angela Celano now.'

I smiled at her. 'We got a game of chess on.'

'Hi Nick.' She stood and they shook hands. 'Old Nick, huh.'

'Nice to meet you, but hey, don't get too personal ... they don't call me that no more.' We all chuckled.

'You spoke very well at the funeral.'

'Thank you ... Mrs. Celano.'

He rubbed his temple. 'Debono? Where have I heard that name?' I knew he was struggling. Nick's memory lets him down sometimes, just like mine.

'I'll explain later. We'll be done in ten,' I said.

'Sure mate.' And he headed back out to the kitchen, still scratching his head.

She picked up a castle from Nick's marble chess set, as always, laid out on the board carved into the coffee table in front of us.

'So he ended up teaching you how to play chess, too?'

'Can't beat him, though.'

'He's doing all right for a dead man.'

'Full of surprises, our Nick.'

'How did he—?'

'Now there's a story. One of my most cherished memories is the joy on Jack's face when he brought him home. Those first three years in St Claire were the toughest for Jack until shortly after his eighteenth birthday. He and Wendy were driving his new car along the Great Ocean Road on a cloudy day, when suddenly he skidded and pulled up at a lookout. Wendy reckons poor Rex was nearly thrown through the windscreen. Jack fled from the car and couldn't get his eyes off the sight out to sea. A large ground swell was running and he pointed to a solitary figure in the distance taking off down a wave. He knew the style, the board, the crouched stance and the arms out like seagull's wings as he carved across the face, just like Jack said in his writing. Turns out Nick couldn't get the car started that horrible day of the Ash Wednesday fires, but there was an old bike in the shed. He knew the danger and tucked his board under his arm and rode to the ocean before the fire turned. Spent five hours sitting on his board in the sea with a tee shirt over his head in order to survive the smoke.

'He worked for me and lived with my wife and I for several years.'

She tapped the folder. 'Jack must have been devastated when he wrote this, before he found Nick again.'

'He spent a lot of time in his room when we first moved to St Claire. My wife and I were worried sick.'

'Jack really looked up to him.'

'They had this special relationship, like he had two fathers. Nick will always have a home, Jack made sure of that. Now he lives here, in Jack and Wendy's beach house with Cherub, his partner.'

She smiled. 'I'm old fashioned. Never called my husband a partner.'

'Me too.'

'Did Nick clear everything up ... with the police?'

'Jack did. Legalised him, as he liked to call the process. Some years after he got Nick a lawyer and they all went to court in Brisbane. Jack in his twisted humour reckons he did it because Nick needed a passport so they could go on surfing trips to Indonesia together. He got a twelve-month good behaviour bond with no conviction for the assault. They let him return to Victoria immediately. Also received a backhanded apology from the Judge who agreed he should never have been conscripted in the first place. No one should have, he said. Bottomly also cleared him of any involvement in the disappearance of your brother.'

'I know. He tried to re-open the case back in the mid-nineties. They requested DNA samples from the other boys involved. To try and match the cigarette butts. A court refused. The evidence could only point to them burying a dead sheep.' Her phone rang and she pressed a button on the screen but didn't answer. 'Listen, I have to go. With your permission, can

I keep this and work on it? I'll have something for you very soon and we can discuss where we go from there.'

'Okay,' I said. 'But please, be respectful. I trust you to keep me in the loop. I want your word on that. There's stuff in there about Wendy and Jack.'

'Of course you have my word. I thought it was cute. He didn't take Hans's advice about not marrying his first girlfriend.'

'No one ever took Hans's advice on anything.'

She gave her caring smile, squeezed my hands again and stood to leave. 'We'll do this together.'

I nodded. 'If you need money—'

'It's fine, I know people. I'll be in touch, Mr. Gillings, err John. It's been good … catching up, again. I'm sorry for your loss.'

'Okay. Thank you.' I held the door for her and watched her leave down the stairs, but I wasn't finished until I asked her. 'Hey.'

She stopped midway and turned.

'There's something I have to know. All this aside, I need to know what you really think of Jack. After what he did.'

Her lips flattened out in thought. 'I used to watch him through the front window riding his bike. Jack was the little brother I always wanted to have. Despite everything, I just remember a boy and his dog trying to get by in a big world. Like all of us.'

I think it took me about a minute to muster a reply. By that time she was gone.

'So do I,' I muttered.

I closed the door and sat down, waiting for Nick, wondering if I'd done the right thing or not. Then I thought of the email and knew it was what he really wanted. I looked at those marble chess pieces in front, all set up for our game and my mind spiralled back to last Christmas when I heard Nick's prophecy from the book for the first time. Jack was sitting where I am now playing chess with Nick. They liked to try and prod and put each other off their game as best they could. Jack made a smartarse comment, I've forgotten what it was, but Nick didn't take too kindly to it and grabbed Jack in one of those long armed headlocks and said, "I told you once, no matter who you are, no matter how much money you got, son. Always remember, at the end of the game all the kings and queens and pawns go back in the same box." The next day Jack found the lump.

PETER EDWARDS

A final word from me.

I wrote this book because our governments will never have the fortitude to hold them fully accountable. Sadly that's a knowledge, not just a belief.

Follow me on instagram

peteredwardsallmine

Like my book, then please like my page

www.facebook.com/PeterEdwardsAuthor/

Twitter: Peter Edwards@allminestories

Website: allminestories.com

Email: allminestories@bigpond.com

PETER EDWARDS

Acknowledgements.

My dearest thanks to my early readers, Olivia Scott, Anne and Dave Blackie, Trevor Oxley, John Fawcett, Julie Rennie, Jude Reeves, Caity Cantwell, Lisa Edward, Chris Haddock and Paul and Bronwyn Bliszczyk. Thank you for your confidence and feedback. You have all contributed immensely to the final outcome.

In loving memory of Tim Howells.
Unfortunately Tim didn't get to read this work, but I will never forget his friendship throughout my life and his encouragement toward my early writing.
Rest in peace my friend.

Thank you to Dave and Anne Blackie who provided a thought provoking discussion (as always over sav blanc and beer), resulting in the fine-tuning of the epilogue of this book.

To author, Julie Rennie. Many thanks for your help in publishing this extract and your work on finding me the right cover designer, and also for your patience and general advice on publishing.

Thank you to my wonderful editor, Serena Sandrin-Tatti. Without your guidance, criticism, patience, command of the English language and amazing encouragement, this work would not have been possible. Mistakes are mine. I own them.

Pete.

ALL MINE

By Peter Edwards

Part 1
Murder,
And The
Homecoming

1

Coogee, Sydney

Welham woke to that incessant, awful rattle only hard plastic vibrating on a glass table can make. He reached out, fumbling blindly onto one handset. The buzzing continued until his hand slapped down on the second phone just as the noise ceased. He flipped the top open, raised his sunnies and waited for his eyes to adjust. Blurred words became crisp.

A missed call from a private number, he knew it was Ingliss.

He rubbed his eyes, yawning. Down below the chatter of Coogee beachgoers rose on the soft sea breeze that had kicked in while he slept. Wind also tickled the chimes on the neighbouring balcony. Welham was yet to meet the new couple who'd moved into the apartment only a week ago. Shooting the string on their annoying ornament was probably a little premature. A slight mention about the chimes and the fact he was on the building's body corp committee – while they waited at the lift – would be more appropriate.

Behind him the balcony door slid open.

'Went inside, you were snoring,' Tracey said.

'I'm rooted. Really needed that little snooze.'

'Whose phone was that, sweetie?'

'Mine.'

She lifted her mobile off the table, checked it and took it back inside.

Matching phones. What next?

Such a delightful woman, yet so many annoying traits. Just last week she needed a new phone and bought the same model as his, a Motorola. *"They looked cute together,"* had been her comment.

Another sharp vibration in his palm. Sunlight forced him to angle the screen to read the blunt text from Ingliss.

—PICK UP BENSON AWAIT FURTHER ORDERS—

Ingliss was still pressing ahead with surveillance. Three days ago they received a tip off. A container carrying Mexican cocaine would be moved off the Botany Bay wharves today, placing detectives from Strikeforce Phoenix, Federal Police and Australian Customs on full alert. Yet the shipment had not been located, it was now late Sunday afternoon. Welham had hoped for an easy night, suspecting it had already been moved or might not even exist at all.

Glancing over his shoulder to make sure the door was closed, he rang Ingliss and confirmed he was about to leave, then called his partner. Benson answered.

'It's Welham. Be ready in fifteen.'

'Yeah, just got the message.'

He was about to hang up when he detected Benson's puffing. A high-pitched voice hung in the background.

'Carn Daddy, hurry up n' bowl.'

'We interrupting cricket again?' Welham said. Each time he visited, Benson's son Jake tried to rope him into a game.

'It's stinking hot, can't get the cheatin' little shit out.'

Welham chuckled. 'Get yourself fit old son.'

'That train's left the station mate, see you when you get here.'

Welham snapped the handset shut. Stiffness made him groan as he hauled himself up off the sun lounge, a reminder of the *"welcome to the back nine"* card he received from his golfing mates on his recent fortieth. Inside, he filled a glass of water and switched the air conditioner off.

'What 'ya do that for?' Tracey said. She was lying on the couch, facing away, typing into her new phone.

'Off to work.'

'Seriously, this late, thought we were doing dinner?' She held up her empty glass. 'Be a darling.'

He grabbed a fresh wine bottle from the fridge, carried it over and jammed it in the ice bucket on the coffee table, then quickly shoved it under her bikini top.

Squealing loudly, she jumped up holding the phone at arm's length. The bottle tumbled onto the carpet. 'You're so going to pay for that,' she said, half seriously through a tensed jaw, flicking icy droplets off her chest.

'Have to get you moving somehow,' he said, laughing. 'Take it with you.'

'Can't I stay? My place'll be roasting.'

'Go to the beach.'

'Can't be stuffed.'

Earlier in the day she whinged about her air conditioner playing up again, he felt a little sorry for her. She lived in a rented apartment, west side of the building four doors down the road.

'What about dinner?' Tracey asked, gathering her clothes. 'How long will you be?'

'Who knows, I'll call if I feel like something.'

'We should try the new Greek place on Dolphin Street.'

'Along with every other arsehole in Coogee. Maybe during the week when it's quieter.' He wandered off to his room, strapped on his holster, checked his gun, changed into better shorts, a shirt and boat shoes without socks. When he returned to the main room Tracey waited by the door, her handbag was slung over a shoulder, the ice bucket and wine nestled in her other arm.

They kissed.

Eyes followed her to the elevator. He tapped his pockets, felt only keys, his wallet, no phone, and he couldn't see it on the outside table where he thought it was. Instead he found it on the coffee table beside the small pool of water from the ice bucket. With no time to wipe up he locked the door and left.

———

The traffic lightened as Coogee trailed off behind. When he arrived at Benson's Newtown address, young Jake sprinted out the front door and across the lawn around to the driver's side. Welham dug into the ashtray for a coin.

'Hey Craig,' Jake said through a gap-toothed grin, elbows stretched uncomfortably up through the open window.

Welham shook his hand. 'Getting stronger little man.'

'Yup, sure am.' He focussed on Welham's left hand.

'Been helping your mum?'

'Yup, doing what she asks.'

He winked, handing over two-dollars. 'Remember the deal?'

'I know, don't tell the old man.' The wink came back.

'Good boy.'

Benson's wife appeared carrying a bag to her car.

'What's your mission soldier?'

'Going to Grandma's, Daddy says you're coming for dinner.'

'Is that so?'

Benson climbed into the passenger seat, placing a camera bag in the back.

'Get going buddy,' Benson said to Jake, 'see you later if you're still up.'

'Sure Dad, bye Craig.' He raced away with the coin clutched in his fist.

'Got plans tonight,' Welham said, driving off.

'Come on, you're leaving this week, Mum's worried, might never see you again.'

'She'll find me. What if we're late?'

'Few expansion cracks in the gravy, plastic tasting veges, nothin' that'll kill ya, least it'll be warm.'

'Guess I'm locked in,' Welham said.

His partner's mobile rang. Benson took the call and listened. 'We're on the move, I'll put him on.' He held his hand over the microphone. 'It's Ingliss. He called before. Head to the Norfolk Arms Hotel, Botany Road, I'll fill you in on the way.' He passed the handset to Welham.

'Detective, why can't I reach you? Been trying your number,' his boss said.

'No Idea.' Welham glanced down at his own phone face up on the console, turned on. Radio silence had been ordered for the operation. 'You brass keep telling us how good this new digital system is. Who am I to argue.'

'Just hurry up, get to that pub, Purcell and Cornes need to be relieved.'

'Only a few minutes away.'

'Good.' Ingliss hung up.

Welham passed the mobile back and picked his own up. 'What's he on about? Got five bars of reception.'

Welham turned onto Botany Road, dropped Benson off a block away and parked across from the Norfolk Arms Hotel.

Once inside, he bought a beer, shouldered his way back through the crowd and found a quiet space beside the front window. Memories of younger days sprung to mind, bluing wharfies, live music, nicotine clouds at eye level. Walls now had a fresh coat. Gold stars dotted the carpet leading to an opaque glass door separating the pokies.

Detective Cornes sat at a table next to the back wall. Purcell stood at the bar. When he saw Welham, he drained his beer and walked outside where he met Benson on the smokers' deck. They chatted like old mates before Benson entered, heading straight to the betting counter where he studied a form guide pinned to the felt wall. He scribbled on a betting ticket, crossed it out, marked up another card and took it to the bar, paid for his bet, bought a beer.

Welham moved quickly to the betting counter, lifted the first ticket, turned it over and read Benson's scribble on the back — *pool table, red tee shirt, dark hair, glasses.* Over the other side of the bar, pool balls cracked from an opening break.

Welham picked out a short figure with familiar thick lips, puffy, olive cheeks, oily hair. He wore a red polo with ripples in the collar, warped at the hem by a perfect potbelly. He looked harder to make sure.

Little fat Joey Avola was lining up the white ball.

What are you doing in Sydney? Welham thought.

Purcell's partner Bruce Cornes left. Several minutes later a woman at the bar smiled, half attractive, her better days gone by. Welham strolled over and struck up a conversation, ignoring Benson's glare from the end of the bar. Avola moved to a corner, answered his phone and plugged a finger in the opposite ear. Welham caught the sudden rise of his partner's brow before Benson departed through a side door. The woman mentioned live music in the bar later that evening. Welham concentrated over her shoulder, Avola left through the main door.

'Got to go.' He downed his pot. 'Music starts at nine, yeah?'

'You'll be here?'

'Sounds good.' He needed an excuse, Benson's mother dished up crap.

Outside, his partner stood impatiently at the driver's door, a hand stretched. 'Hurry the fuck up.'

Welham tossed the keys, they settled into traffic, south bound towards Botany Bay.

'The white van,' said Benson.

'Name's Joey Avola.'

'Know him?'

'Family's known, crossed em' years ago.'

'That all I get? From Sydney?'

'Griffith. Don't lose him.'

'Mafia?'

'Family's connected, Joey's the try-hard.'

'Try-hard, huh. Just like you. What the hell were you doing in there, anyway?'

'Surveillance.'

Benson shook his head.

'Oh come on Sammy, she was passable. You're just jealous women don't hit on you, those hairy guardrails on that bald scone of yours, scare the bejesus out of anyone.'

'I'm happily married, dipshit. What about Tracey?'

'Who?'

'Tracey ... Tracey, fuck you're a moron sometimes. Settle down instead of tappin' anything breathing. She gets along with the missus for Christ's sake, must be all right.'

'They've met once.'

'First impressions work on my wife. I know.'

Welham laughed. 'Always thinking of yourself.'

Benson returned a hot glare. 'You can talk, when will you man up?'

'Don't go there mate, Tracey's an okay chick, not the be all, monogamy's not for everyone.'

'Yeah, right, sooner you stop referring to women as *"okay chicks"* and start treating 'em like real ladies. I warn ya, don't speak around my wife like that.'

Welham's mobile rang. 'Working again,' he said, glad to be rid of the subject. He answered.

'Detective Welham. Superintendent Mersche. Your exact location, please?'

'Botany Road, we just passed the airport. The man we're tailing is Joey Avola—'

'Let him go.'

'What? Does Ingliss know?'

'You have your orders, Detective. Inspector Ingliss is in a briefing as we speak. Janis cannot be compromised. Another team will pick him up.

Welham listened to Mersche's further instructions and hung up, staring off to the right. Clumsy looking, towering red dock cranes never failed to remind him of Tripods from John Christopher's Tripod trilogy he'd read as a boy.

He thought about calling Ingliss, but Mersche was right. Operation Janus, the largest organised crime investigation ever undertaken in Australia, was poised to commence within a week. Welham's team would re-ignite investigations into Italian businesses and superannuation funds throughout the Riverina district of Southern New South Wales. 'Gotta let him go, Sam.'

'Serious?'

'Orders, mate.'

'This to do with your little upgrade?'

'Yeah.'

'Be fucked if I'm calling you sir.'

'Day's coming, smartarse. Left into this business park up ahead, before the roundabout.'

Benson grinned as they entered through black iron gates onto a common driveway, paved with serrated bricks the colour of sunburnt skin.

Welham pointed. 'Head right, looking for Asian Pacific Logistic Solutions.'

They drove down the business park between reflective glass offices, freight terminals and warehouses. Long trailers minus the rigs rested on front hydraulic legs in the centre island of the commonway. No other cars visible.

'That's it there.' Welham pointed to the letters A. P. L. S. on the roller door. 'Get a visual.'

They found one, five buildings away. Benson reversed beneath cantilevered offices and cut the ignition.

ATTENTO SEAFOODS TERMINAL FOUR was sprawled in block across the roller door of the warehouse directly opposite.

'What are we looking for?' Benson asked, reaching behind for the camera bag.

'Don't know yet.' Minutes later a canary yellow transit van pulled up at A.P.L.S. The driver remained inside. Benson fitted a long lens and began snapping. Welham reached into his pocket for a notebook. Benson read out the number plate.

'What's he doing?'

'Fuck all,' said Benson.

'Recognise him?'

'Nuh.'

Movement came, up in a window on the second level of Attento Seafoods. Welham concentrated hard, only a glint of sunlight bounced back. He returned his focus to the van. The driver hadn't moved. A glass door in the front of Attento Seafoods opened. A man appeared wheeling a luggage bag, tall, thick set, jet-black hair. With his back to them, he twisted keys in the door. A navy blue office shirt fluttered between broad shoulders, a lengthy black coat was draped over his left arm. Mascot Airport was less than two kilometres away. Welham assumed he was an executive ready to fly out to a colder climate. The man walked off toward the end of the court. Welham saw only the side profile of the face, he disappeared behind a parked trailer with a blue shipping container on the back. Benson's camera clicked furiously. The driver now stood at the side door of the yellow van.

'Com'on you piece o' shit, turn around,' Benson said. Only the driver's back was visible. 'Might have to get closer.'

'Wait'll this guy pisses off.' Welham looked toward the far end of the trailer, expecting the executive to appear. Instead, he stepped out from the front corner, the bag and coat gone.

Instantly Welham recognised the face. Carlo Caruso marched forward, black-gloved hands grasping a dark muzzle.

'Get down,' Welham yelled, sparks flew, bullets pinged off the bonnet puncturing the windscreen. He wrenched his gun out, slid down, another volley strafed the car, squares of glass and bullets rained, thumping the seat above his head.

The firing ceased.

His heart thrashed. Lungs heaved, gasping frantically. He was alive.

Benson's chin rested, dead. Welham let off six rounds up through the vacant screen. No fire returned. He raised his head, far as he dared. Silence. Was Caruso down? He found the door handle; it clicked open, a stream of bullets thundered into the outer skin. Metal ripped metal, bullets spat and bounced. Many others penetrated.

———

Carlo released his finger. A mild puff of smoke drifted from the insulated silencer of the MAC 10, yet it felt cool to the touch. The Mexicans were right about the powerful muzzle climb. Thousand bullets a minute, they said.

The passenger's left arm twitched. A finger lifted. Carlo eased the Glock from his belt, fired into the side of the head, then slipped the pistol back and crossed the commonway towards Reynolds, the driver of the yellow van. The roller door of A.P.L.S. let out an oil deprived screech as it slid up to reveal the truck. The engine turned over, the truck shook, idling.

Reynolds' empty hands hung at his side. Sweat beaded like shingles on his forehead.

'Who's in the truck?'

'Your replacement.'

'No, Carlo … we had a deal.' A hand moved to his back.

Carlo fired, relishing in the man's disbelieving gaze.

He studied the weapon. Impressive.

The man hired to kill him took the full impact of at least fifteen bullets, perhaps in under a second. He made a circling motion above his head. The truck shunted forward over the body.

allminestories@bigpond.com